A Map

of the

CITY OF WASHINGTON

in the District of Columbia

established as the permanent Seat of the Government

of the

United States

OF AMERICA

taken from actual Survey, as laid out
on the Ground

by N. King
Surveyor of the City of Washington

East Front of the Capitol of the United States

Publication of this book was made possible through
a generous grant from the

VERIZON FOUNDATION
http://foundation.verizon.com

Where the People Speak

The United States Capitol and Its Place in American History

Andrew R. Dodge

PUBLISHED BY
UNITED STATES CAPITOL HISTORICAL SOCIETY
WASHINGTON, D. C.

Photographs and maps courtesy of the Office of Architect of the Capitol, Office of
the Senate Curator, the Library of Congress, Massachusetts Historical Society,
New-York Historical Society, Historical Society of Pennsylvania, U.S. Geological
Survey, Cornell University Library, and the National Park Service.

Library of Congress Cataloguing-in-Publication Data

Dodge, Andrew R., 1947-

Where the People Speak:
The United States Capitol and Its Place in American History

Includes bibliography and index.
ISBN #0-916200-32-9
LC call number in process

Contents

COURTESY OF USCHS

The Capitol Dome through the years: At bottom, William Thornton's original design, which pleased George Washington, featured a low, restrained Dome. By the mid-19th century, at center, it had grown, the result of Charles Bulfinch's redesign. Finally, as rebuilt in the late 1850s and early 1860s, at top, the Dome, as designed by Thomas U. Walter, achieves its familiar shape and size.

Preface

The United States Capitol:
The Symbol and Heart of American Democracy

The United States government is one of the oldest democracies in the world, and the U.S. Capitol is recognized around the globe as a symbol of freedom and self-rule. It is the home of the oldest and most important branch of this nation's government, the Congress. The Capitol is the building where our directly elected national representatives meet to debate and to pass legislation for the American people. This is where the people speak and where all points of view can be freely expressed.

Shortly after the first European settlers arrived in North America in the 1600s, people began to establish representative organizations as forums to discuss issues of concern and to make laws to govern themselves. The Mayflower Compact, the document the Pilgrims signed upon their arrival in Massachusetts in

Mayflower Pilgrims begin the process of self-government: The Mayflower Compact that they signed on November 21, 1620, was a set of rules to help them establish a new community. For years it served as the constitution of the Plymouth Colony.

1620, marked the first time a group of people created a framework for the establishment of a government in which the people would elect individuals to enact laws for the benefit and good of all the people.

When the colonists rebelled against what they considered British oppression during the 18th century, American society chose leaders who had to create an entire set of institutions and attempt to develop a unified national identity. Since the beginning of our national representative form of government more than 200 years ago, the nation has progressed from the First Continental Congress, comprised of European American males, into the Congress we know today, with members from a wide range of racial and ethnic backgrounds representing a population of approximately 300 million citizens, a rich and diverse people with ancestral ties to almost every area of the world.

Just as Congress evolved, the idea of a federal city and a national Capitol went through a similar process before becoming a reality. During the Revolutionary years and after the adoption of the Articles of Confederation on March 1, 1781, Congress met in buildings provided by local and state governments. Not until 1800 did the federal government move into its own home under the sole jurisdiction of Congress.

Since 1800, when the national government moved from Philadelphia, Pennsylvania, to the new federal district, now known as Washington, D.C., Congress has always met in the Capitol. When Congress arrived, only the Senate wing was ready for its new occupants. In August 1814, before the Capitol was completed, British troops paid an unwelcome visit to Washington during the War of 1812 and burned the Capitol along with many other buildings, including the White House, then called the President's Mansion. The Capitol sustained major damage in the fire, and it took two decades to repair and finally complete the building. In the 1850s, the Capitol went through an extensive rebuilding to make room for future members and to accommodate the needs of a growing nation.

Some may look at the United States Capitol and see nothing more than a large, imposing white building made of marble with a cast-iron Dome, but this is only the outward symbol of our democratic institutions. Most importantly, the Capitol is the home of Congress, which traces its roots through our country's history of successes and failures from the very origins of our nation and embodies a living link to the Founding Fathers. It also serves as a museum, displaying paintings and statues that commemorate great events and leaders throughout our nation's history. Those works of art give us an insight into how we have viewed ourselves during the past 200 years.

"When in the Course of Human Events"

1774-1790

CONGRESS: 1763-1790

With the conclusion of the French and Indian War in 1763, the British government set in motion a plan for a new economic and political relationship with its colonies in North America. Britain had spent tremendous amounts of money to defeat the French in military engagements, ranging from those in the Americas and Europe to some as far east as India. The British wanted the American colonies to pay what they considered the colonies' fair share of the debt and began imposing taxes similar to those the English paid.

Through this policy, the British government commenced a series of actions that would ultimately lead to revolution. The two sources of conflict between the American colonies and Britain centered on how money was to be raised and the Proclamation Line of 1763, which called for the garrisoning of British Army units in the colonies to stop westward expansion and to remove all settlements west of the Appalachian Mountains. The Proclamation

Standing tall and proud and flanked by members of his committee, which had been charged with drafting a Declaration of Independence, Thomas Jefferson presents the document to the Continental Congress in July 1776.

Line impacted the aspirations and long-term goals of many Americans who wanted to move west and develop new territories, but the tax issue was the most immediate and affected the largest percentage of the population.

Because of ignorance and arrogance, the leadership in London did not understand the social and political structures in America and wanted to impose laws and taxes directly on the colonies. On the other side of the Atlantic Ocean, the representative bodies in each of the colonies felt they should be the ones to decide how to raise money. This contentious period, with the British imposition of increasingly onerous taxes and acts, pushed many in the colonies to seek redress and a restoration of their relationship with Britain to that which existed before the French and Indian War.

That political struggle marked the origin of an American government and the starting point in the history of the development of a national capital and the Capitol building. Those on the side of colonial self-rule did not see themselves as revolutionaries creat-

FIRST CONTINENTAL CONGRESS
Carpenters' Hall,
Philadelphia, Pennsylvania
September 5, 1774 – October 26, 1774

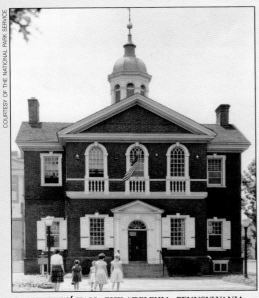

CARPENTERS' HALL, PHILADELPHIA, PENNSYLVANIA

Representatives met in Carpenters' Hall, Philadelphia, Pennsylvania, on September 5, 1774, and adjourned on October 26,1774. This was the first national meeting of delegates, and all the colonies sent representatives—except Georgia. Georgia's absence was a reflection of some of the complex issues that prevailed during this period. Although many Georgians supported the call for the meeting, a majority wished to avoid offending the British in the summer of 1774 in the hope of getting the British Army to help them fight a frontier war against the Creek Indians. The assembled delegates petitioned Parliament under the Declaration of Colonial Rights to restore colonial legislative prerogatives, to guarantee the rights of liberty, property, and trial by jury, and to repeal the Intolerable Acts. Congress also established a trade embargo against Britain, attempting to force business interests there to pressure Parliament to stop interfering in the colonies.

TIME LINE   ☆ *Louis XVI, who would be the first head of state to recognize the United States, became king of France in May 1774.*

ing a movement toward independence. They would be considered reactionaries who only sought to reestablish the prewar relationship of self-rule. To work toward that goal, delegates from each of the colonies decided to meet in Philadelphia during September 1774, the first time that the colonies met as a national government. Massachusetts called for the meeting to take place in Philadelphia, and only Georgia, which did not wish to offend the British for internal security reasons, went unrepresented.

The objective of this meeting, now known as the First Continental Congress, was simple, and the message sent to the crown was written in a conciliatory manner. The Declaration of Colonial Rights succinctly set forth the request that all colonists be guaranteed personal and property rights, that the newly passed British trade restrictions be repealed, and that all powers be restored to the colonial assemblies. The message concluded with a warning to the crown of unpleasant consequences if Parliament and the king's ministers did not heed the colonists' wishes. From

SECOND CONTINENTAL CONGRESS
State House,
Philadelphia, Pennsylvania
May 10, 1775 – December 12, 1776

Since the First Continental Congress failed to receive "a redress of grievances," members met a second time. As a result of Britain's failure to respond and the fact that the Revolutionary War had already commenced, Congress felt compelled to issue the Declaration of Independence. By this action, Congress assumed all the responsibilities of governing. Members abandoned their temporary capitol in the face of advancing British troops under the command of Lord Charles Cornwallis and moved to Baltimore, Maryland, in December 1776.

STATE HOUSE, PHILADELPHIA, PENNSYLVANIA

☆ *British troops defeated Patriots at the Battle of Bunker (Breed's) Hill, June 17, 1775.*

the time of that first national meeting in 1774, a new form of government would come into being in America and evolve into the government we know today. The colonial leaders did not possess a road map to direct them in dealing with the British. Once they determined to seek independence, they had to face the more difficult problem of organizing a national government.

The colonial leaders met the first challenge within two years by issuing the Declaration of Independence, but in so doing, they faced the almost insurmountable task of defeating the foremost military and economic power in the world at that time. If and when they might be successful in winning independence, the Founding Fathers would be confronted with the even more difficult challenge of creating a new, stable, and lasting government.

During the Revolution and the formative years of the republic, the Founding Fathers had to deal with fighting a war and establishing a national government while having to move from one place to another. They had to rely upon the hospitality of state and

SECOND CONTINENTAL CONGRESS
Henry Fite's House,
Baltimore, Maryland
December 20, 1776 – March 4, 1777

Baltimore, now in the midst of winter, had few of the amenities members had enjoyed in Philadelphia, and they found living in the city an unpleasant burden. Making matters worse, the war was not going well. In this environment, Congress gave George Washington unparalleled powers to create an army, seize property, and arrest dissenters during the first six months of 1777.

HENRY FITE'S HOUSE, BALTIMORE, MARYLAND

SECOND CONTINENTAL CONGRESS
State House,
Philadelphia, Pennsylvania
March 4, 1777 – September 18, 1777

Congress was relieved by Washington's military successes in New Jersey during December, and members were delighted to be able to return to the pleasures and comfort of Philadelphia. However, the mood soon changed. Congress' continued effort to support the Continental Army achieved only the modest results of retaining just 4,000 soldiers, and the nation faced looming British attacks from Canada and another advance on Philadelphia. During this short stay, the members did resolve to create a national flag with each of the 13 states represented by an individual star on a blue field and 13 alternating red and white stripes.

TIME LINE   ☆ *Washington crossed the Delaware River and defeated the British at Trenton and Princeton, New Jersey, December 1776.*

local jurisdictions for meeting places. Between 1774 and the establishment of a permanent home for the Capitol in 1800, the various Congresses moved 14 times and met in 8 different cities before the final move to the new federal district along the Potomac River.

Since there were none of the modern conveniences we take for granted today, these meetings and moves placed a real hardship on the representatives. Philadelphia was a natural choice because of its central location. It had the largest population in the Americas and one of the largest in the British Empire. It provided the best amenities of any 18th century American city. Other cities where they met, such as Baltimore, York, and Lancaster, were comprised of only a few hundred buildings and had populations only a fraction the size of Philadelphia's.

In Baltimore, for example, delegates brought along their wives in order to have some semblance of a social life. The city woefully lacked the amenities that Philadelphia offered. Delegates had to pay for expensive accommodations at taverns and private

COURT HOUSE, YORK, PENNSYLVANIA

SECOND CONTINENTAL CONGRESS
Court House, Lancaster, Pennsylvania
September 27, 1777

Beating a hasty retreat from Philadelphia after the Continental Army's defeat at the Battle of Brandywine, Congress met in the second largest town in the state to contend with pressing military issues, to secure the treasury, and to vote to move further west to the safety of York, Pennsylvania, across the Susquehanna River.

SECOND CONTINENTAL CONGRESS
Court House, York, Pennsylvania
September 30, 1777 – June 27, 1778

Congress achieved two major goals while meeting in York. Ever since the First Continental Congress, the delegates had been working without any written charter to set forth the powers or relationship of the Congress with the people and the states. Initially drafted early in July 1776, the Articles of Confederation remained in a committee and was a persistent source of debate. Finally, in November 1777, Congress agreed to submit the Articles to the states for ratification. The second important event occurred on February 6, 1778, when the King of France, Louis XVI, signed a treaty of military alliance with the colonies. On May 4, 1778, Congress ratified another treaty of alliance with France titled, "Amity and Commerce."

☆ *During October 1777, an American army stopped a British invasion from Canada. Washington wintered at Valley Forge, Pennsylvania, 1777 – 1778.*

homes, which led one disgruntled delegate to refer to Baltimore as an "extravagant hole," reflecting the lack of liquor and the high cost of rooms.

In addition to enduring the normal inconveniences of the 18th century, including poor food, undesirable rooms, and the hardships of taking days to travel from one town to another by horse, cart, or carriage over rough dirt or mud roads in all seasons of the year, many of the delegates suffered personally and financially.

Besides the common afflictions brought on by aging, a number of delegates, such as Samuel Chase of Maryland and George Walton of Georgia, suffered from gout, commonly associated with too much rich food and alcohol. Abraham Clark of New Jersey had to contend with the fact that the British had captured his sons while they were serving with the Continental Army. A number of the other delegates, such as George Clymer of Pennsylvania, William Hooper of North Carolina, and John Hart of New Jersey, had their homes destroyed during the war or faced financial ruin.

SECOND CONTINENTAL CONGRESS
College Hall and State House,
Philadelphia, Pennsylvania
July 2, 1778 – March 1, 1781

After spending almost a year in the city, British forces withdrew toward New York. The occupation had rendered most public buildings and homes uninhabitable because they had been used as barracks and stables, with horse manure disposed of in basements. When Congress arrived, members found that they could not meet in the State House and decided to convene temporarily in College Hall, part of the College of Philadelphia. The Congress' first order of business on July 9, 1778, was to formally present the Articles of Confederation, Maryland created a delay by demanding a settlement of the western land issue. Although Maryland had no land entitlements, it wanted to settle the

western territorial claims of other states, which originated in their charters. Under several of the charters, states held conflicting claims to vast territories that extended to the Mississippi River. The final agreement that Congress later accepted became the foundation for the admission of all future territories and states.

SECOND CONTINENTAL CONGRESS
State House,
Philadelphia, Pennsylvania
March 1, 1781 – June 21, 1783

On March 1, 1781, Maryland finally agreed to the Articles, and the United States of America came into existence as a formal government with a written charter. This was a major milestone in the development of republican democracy. Although fatally flawed in its not granting Congress the power to control the nation's finances and

---

TIME LINE   ☆ *After crushing defeats at King's Mountain and Cowpens, South Carolina, in 1780-1781, British troops moved toward Yorktown, Virginia, where Lord Cornwallis surrendered on October 19, 1781.*

Other delegates faced sickness and death. In 1775, while attending the Second Continental Congress, John Adams received news that his brother had died of dysentery, and later that year, his wife, Abigail, wrote him, "I have passed thro great distress both of Body and mind. I was seaz'd with [dysentery] in a violent manner. Our Little Tommy. . . lies very ill now—there is no abatement . . . of his disorder . . . Our House is an hospital in every part." She noted that many in the community suffered from smallpox. The death of Maryland delegate Thomas Stone's wife from complications resulting from a smallpox vaccination kept him from attending the Constitutional Convention in 1787. Others, like William Hooper of North Carolina, had to resign for health or financial reasons, and Philip Livingston of New York died on June 12, 1778, while attending the congressional session in York, Pennsylvania.

The Founding Fathers overcame the adversities of life, war, and sectional differences to create a new national government. Even though it took years and they had to rely upon the gracious-

trade issues, the Articles enabled the national government to raise an army but failed to provide the means for funding it. The Congress also discussed peace terms with the British to formally end the Revolutionary War. The session ended abruptly when an angry group of Continental soldiers demanded to be paid and joined in what became known as the "Philadelphia Mutiny." Fearing violence, the members fled to Princeton, New Jersey.

CONFEDERATION CONGRESS
Prospect Hall and Nassau Hall, Princeton, New Jersey
June 30, 1783 – November 4, 1783

After escaping from the mutiny in Philadelphia, Alexander Hamilton and the other delegates debated the issue of a permanent home for the Congress and its possible locations. Before adjourning, Congress agreed to alternate meeting places between Annapolis, Maryland, and Trenton, New Jersey, until the establishment of a permanent capital. This session also marked the beginning of successive meetings of Congress when it failed to have a quorum to conduct business. Many members believed that since the war was over, there was no longer any need for a national government.

NASSAU HALL, PRINCETON, NEW JERSEY

☆ *The Peace of Paris, which ended the Revolutionary War, was signed on September 3, 1783.*

ness of states to offer a place for the Congress to meet between 1774 and 1800, the delegates and members were always able to advance their cause. Not unlike today, there were times when the representatives were the embodiment of statesmanship and rose above politics, but at other times, members effectively utilized political maneuvering to achieve their ends, as Alexander Hamilton did in pressing for a strong central government.

Hamilton played a crucial role in major events that would lead to the establishment of a federal government. He envisioned a governmental structure with the states being subordinated to the national government in key areas, such as finance, trade, and security. To ensure the autonomy of the federal government from state meddling, he sought to establish a capital outside of any state control. As a member of the Confederation Congress, he knew well the shortcomings of the government that the Articles of Confederation had

CONFEDERATION CONGRESS
State House,
Annapolis, Maryland
November 26, 1783 – June 3, 1784

As prescribed by resolution, Congress assembled in Annapolis. The apathy of the states toward the national Congress led to one adjournment after another in November. During the last week of the month, George Washington announced that he was coming to Annapolis in December to resign his command. Washington's resignation was one of the most important events of the period because the general willingly relinquished his commission and thus acknowledged the supremacy of Congress and civilian control of the military. Although the chamber and gallery were filled with observers, only 20 members of Congress, less than

STATE HOUSE, ANNAPOLIS, MARYLAND

half the normal number in attendance during important sessions, were present for the historic event.

TIME LINE ☆ *The last major element of the British Army left American soil, November 25, 1783.*

Beginning in 1790, the Senate met in this room in Congress Hall in Philadelphia. Members enjoyed the comforts of the city while George Washington worked elsewhere to build a permanent capital city.

"Here, sir, the people govern," said Alexander Hamilton (opposite) of the Capitol. He advocated a strong central government and helped broker the compromise that placed Washington, D. C., at its present site.

CONFEDERATION CONGRESS
French Arms Tavern,
Trenton, New Jersey
November 1, 1784 – December 24, 1784

A year had passed since Congress first met in Annapolis, and it was time to return to Trenton. Members were becoming tired of continually moving from place to place. The idea of a permanent seat of government became a major topic of debate. Many proposals called for the creation of a federal district with states contributing funds to build the necessary public buildings. New Jersey delegates lobbied for the new city to be located near Trenton, along the Delaware River; the Pennsylvania delegation sought to have it near the Susquehanna River. Southerners wanted to locate the capital further south,

FRENCH ARMS TAVERN, TRENTON, NEW JERSEY

along the Potomac River. In late December, northern delegates gained a majority, rescinded the rule of going back and forth between Annapolis and Trenton, and passed a resolution to move Congress to New York City.

☆ *Phillis Wheatley, celebrated African American poet, died on December 5, 1784, in Boston, Massachusetts.*

created. His maneuvering for a completely independent federal system of government with its own capital began during June 1783, while Congress was meeting in Philadelphia.

From March 1781 through June 1783, Congress met on the first floor of the State House in Philadelphia, and the state government held its sessions on the second floor. As events developed by mid-1783, Continental soldiers of the Pennsylvania regiments wanted to get paid the money they had been promised during the war. When it became clear that their pay would not be forthcoming, a few soldiers decided to march on the State House on Saturday, June 21, 1783. They selected that date because Congress was not supposed to be in session, and they knew that the state delegation would be meeting. The soldiers thought that since the Congress had no funds and the state had formed the units, approaching the state would be the surest way to get their money. The ensuing confrontation would become known as the "Philadelphia Mutiny."

This tactic was at odds with how Hamilton thought the prob-

CONFEDERATION CONGRESS
City Hall and Fraunce's Tavern, New York, New York
January 11, 1785 – November 4, 1788

CITY HALL, NEW YORK, NEW YORK

Meeting in New York for the first time, Congress continued to debate the location of the national government. Delegates from the North wanted to stay in New York; those from the southern states still pressed for a capital further south.

An unrelated issue, a commerce question, set the stage for settling the debate. As the result of a commerce and navigation dispute between Maryland and Virginia concerning the Potomac River and the Chesapeake Bay, Congress requested the states to send delegates to a special convention in Annapolis on September 11, 1786. Lack of a quorum forced adjournment of the meeting. The failure to even have a quorum brought to a head the general discontent with Congress' powers under the Articles of Confederation, and early in 1787, the states voted to meet in Philadelphia to address congressional authority. Between May 14 and September 17, 1787, the delegates met in closed session and, against the declared purpose of the sessions, wrote the United States Constitution. Delaware was the first state to approve the new document. When New Hampshire became the ninth, the Constitution was ratified. The first constitutional Congress would meet in New York early in 1789.

TIME LINE   ☆ *Congress adopted the Ordinance of 1785, which became the basis for the surveying and sale of public lands.*

Like the Senate, the House of Representatives met in Philadelphia's Congress Hall from 1790 to 1800. The House Speaker conducted business from the raised seat at right.

lem should be resolved because the state would be fulfilling an obligation of the national government. He was adamant that the states should not settle congressional financial obligations and wanted the states to be subservient to Congress. To draw attention to the dangers of a weak national government, he maneuvered members into an emergency session on the day of the protest on the pretext that Congress must prevent the soldiers from breaking into the Federal Bank. When the protesting soldiers arrived, state officials at first rejected their demands. By midday, about 250 men had gathered and started to drink and brandish muskets, causing concern for the delegates inside the State House. Members of Congress arrived in the afternoon and nervously made their way through the gauntlet to get into the building. Even inside they still felt threatened since the soldiers were just outside their windows. Members asked state officials to help quell the disturbance, but they refused.

Later that afternoon, the soldiers and state officials came to a compromise. At about the same time, Congress adjourned but returned that evening and adopted a resolution promoted by Hamilton. It stated that the state's actions were a flagrant affront to the national government, a charge that Pennsylvania officials strongly denied. As a result of the events at the State House, Congress immediately moved to Princeton, New Jersey, and began a debate about establishing a capital that would not depend on the hospitality of any state. The debate served only as the beginning of the process to establish the dominion of the federal government over an area where it would make its permanent home, a concept known as "exclusive jurisdiction."

The State House in Philadelphia, home to Congress from May 10, 1775, to December 12, 1776, was one of many temporary meeting places. Congress spent some 16 years moving from one city to another before deciding in 1790 to build a permanent home.

Leaders, like Hamilton, who wanted a strong central government used the Philadelphia Mutiny to promote the concept that Congress must have supremacy over individual states and absolute control over the place where Congress met. He and others succeeded in pointing out the dangers of relying on a state for the security of Congress. The debate over exclusive jurisdiction began in 1783 and continues to this day regarding the status of Washington, D.C.* As George Washington's secretary of the treasury in 1789, Alexander Hamilton continued his efforts to press for a federal government free from state controls and with each state financially tied to the national government. To achieve his goal, he set to work on an agreement that would become the first major compromise of the new government: the Compromise of 1790. It heralded the beginning of a long series of compromises based on southern fears of being overwhelmed by business and antislavery advocates in the North who posed a threat to the South's slave-based agricultural economy.

* The District of Columbia, with a population of more than 500,000, has no voting members in Congress. However, under the concept of exclusive jurisdiction, some would argue that these residents are represented by all 535 voting members of the House and Senate.

The New Federal City

1790-1792

A CITY FOR THE CAPITOL: THE COMPROMISE OF 1790

After approximately 16 years of moving from one city or town to another, Congress decided that it must find a permanent home. Since the signing of the Peace of Paris, which ended the Revolutionary War in September 1783, the government had moved from Princeton, New Jersey, to Annapolis, Maryland, to Trenton, New Jersey, and then to New York City. Everyone agreed: A permanent location was essential for a stable national government—but where?

Once the Constitutional Convention convened in Philadelphia during May 1787, it became clear that in order to adopt a new system of government, the Articles of Confederation needed to be replaced. Any new document would have to lay out the powers of the central government in a manner flexible enough to be workable for future generations and still provide room for chang-

With George Washington presiding, delegates sign the Constitution in 1787. Benjamin Franklin, with a cane, sits before Washington; Alexander Hamilton is behind Franklin. At the table to Franklin's left is James Madison, chief architect of the document.

ing interpretations as the nation evolved. To achieve this end and to encourage states to ratify the Constitution, many of the articles were left purposefully vague to avoid offending certain states, regions of the country, or segments of the population. The vagueness was evident in Article I, section 8 of the Constitution that dealt with the location and size of the capital city and the powers that Congress could exercise in the new federal enclave. This was done for two reasons: Congress had no precedent to follow, and it did not want to exclude any state or region from the selection process for fear the issue might be seized upon as grounds not to ratify the Constitution.

Some delegates wanted the capital in the North, and some wanted it closer to the South. There were proponents for locating it in one of the big cities, such as New York or Philadelphia, where it would be close to trade and manufacturing interests and away from slavery. Others wanted to insulate Congress from the corrupting influence of money and powerful state interests. As a result, the Constitutional Convention addressed the issue in rather vague language, preferring to leave the matter of deciding the capital's permanent home to the First Congress, which met in March 1789.

Among many other services to his country, George Washington chose the site of the new federal city. The Compromise of 1790 located the capital somewhere along the Potomac River.

Soon after Congress convened its first session in New York City, Federalist Party members quickly opened a new round of debates about establishing a location for the federal government. They based their arguments on Article I, section 8 of the Constitution, which directs Congress: "To exercise exclusive Legislation in all Cases whatsoever, over such District (not exceeding ten Miles square) as may, by Cession of particular States, and the Acceptance of Congress, become the Seat of the Government of the United States."

As the debate continued, so did the lobbying of local, state, and regional leaders to have the capital built in their locality. Alexander Hamilton developed a means to establish a permanent location for the capital city and at the same time to dramatically strengthen the power of the federal government through the Compromise of 1790.

The first part of Hamilton's solution was put forth in the Residence Act, which allowed President George Washington to choose the location for the seat of government along the Potomac River, thus ending all attempts by the northern leadership to have the capital located north of Maryland. As part of the act, the delegates agreed to have the government move to Philadelphia for ten years, which would allow Washington time to locate and build the new city.

The second and equally important part of Hamilton's compromise tied the payment of Revolutionary War debt to the federal treasury. Since the states handed over the responsibility of repaying the debts, each state inherited a vested interest in the financial success of the national government. Although the South decried having to pay other people's debts and the North carped about moving from the comfort and hospitality of an established city to a "howling, malarious, wilderness," both sides accepted the need to compromise in order to settle the two issues.

The site that George Washington selected to build the federal city was between the towns of Georgetown, Maryland, and Alexandria, Virginia. The 10-square mile District would include Georgetown and a large tract of land north of Alexandria. The location Washington chose for the Capitol and the other public buildings was on Maryland's side of the river, near the confluence of the Potomac and the Eastern Branch, also known as the Anacostia River.

When Congress established the federal city, it stated that Congress would have sole rule over the District—"exclusive jurisdiction." This was a direct result of the Philadelphia Mutiny in 1783 and Congress' feeling helpless to control the mob of Continental soldiers. Although the members had no real idea of what exclusive jurisdiction meant, they did know that states would not have any part in governing the District. Until some time shortly after 1800, when the federal government began to assert its control over the District, Congress let citizens of Maryland and Virginia who lived there vote and pay taxes according to the laws of their respective states.

Before Congress could move from Philadelphia in 1800 to the federal district, the Capitol and other government buildings had to be built. George Washington appointed a three-member commission to oversee the design and layout of the buildings and to sell lots to help defray some of the expense of creating the new

"Debate" rages in Congress Hall in a cartoonist's illustration from 1798. Northern states hoped to have the capitol built in their region; southern states in theirs.

city. Washington wanted men who knew the area, who had business experience, and who had a vested interest in ensuring the success of the city.

The first three commissioners were associates of Washington in the Potomac Navigation Company, and they foresaw the economic advantages for the region once the city became established. Dr. David Stuart, one of the commissioners, was a planter who lived near Mount Vernon, George Washington's home. Stuart had the additional advantage of being related to Martha Washington by marriage. The second member was Daniel Carroll of Rock Creek, a member of the powerful Carroll family who founded Maryland in 1634. He owned numerous slaves, several large plantations, one with approximately 4,000 acres, and other large holdings in Montgomery County, Maryland, which bordered the northern side of the new city. Thomas Johnson, the third man in the group, operated a profitable iron works near Frederick, Maryland. He had built Maryland's capitol in Annapolis and he had nominated Washington as commander-in-chief of the Continental Army in 1775.

A 1790 tug of war pits proponents of moving the capitol to Philadelphia on the left against opponents on the right. Speculators riding on the leader's coattails carry bags of the money they expect to make; adversaries complain of the decadence of Philadelphia and the hardships caused by constantly moving.

Thomas Jefferson and others raised questions about the ethics of choosing these men and the entire concept of a strong central government, but Washington was in complete control and had the support of the Federalists and of other prominent leaders, such as James Madison.

As part of the commissioners' mandate to build and develop the city, they set about the task of establishing the boundaries of the District and laying out a city plan. They immediately looked for a surveying team and hired Andrew Ellicott, who, with his men, began surveying the 100-square miles of the District in February 1791.

The commissioners' next and most important duty was to select an individual who could design an entire city and locate the two most important buildings, the Capitol and the President's Mansion. Washington knew a French immigrant who had served in the Revolution, had been wounded during the Battle of Savannah, and was a trained architect and civil engineer. His name was Peter (Pierre) Charles L'Enfant.

Peter L'Enfant's Vision for a New City and Capitol

Born in Paris in 1754, Peter Charles L'Enfant received his training as an architect and civil engineer before coming to America to join the Revolution. A striking individual, six feet tall and with a military and courtly demeanor, L'Enfant provided great service during the war as an engineer and is considered by some to be the Father of the Army Corps of Engineers. He was wounded during the failed attempt to keep the British Army out of Georgia at the Battle of Savannah in 1778, and two years later, he was captured, along with 5,000 soldiers, when the British took control of Charleston, South Carolina. During this period, L'Enfant considered himself to be an American and no longer signed his name Pierre but as Peter L'Enfant.

After the war, L'Enfant moved to New York City and began working as an architect and civil engineer. In 1789, he renovated the building that would become the first official Capitol for the Constitutional Congress, Federal Hall, in Lower Manhattan. It was on the balcony of this building that George Washington took his oath of office and became the first President of the United States on April 30, 1780.

Washington had become impressed with Peter L'Enfant's service to the country during the war, his skills as an engineer, and his talent as an architect. As a result, Washington became L'Enfant's sponsor in March 1791 and recommended him to the commissioners as the most suitable candidate to design the federal city. The commissioners were delighted to follow Washington's suggestion and immediately appointed L'Enfant to plan a new city worthy of the young nation. Thomas Jefferson and the commissioners charged L'Enfant with the duty of not only laying out

French-born engineer Peter Charles L'Enfant served under General Washington during the Revolution; later Washington chose him to design the layout of America's new capital city.

the streets and avenues but also of placing the major public buildings in a harmonious relationship and on suitable sites befitting their importance.

On a clear and beautiful June day in 1791, Washington and L'Enfant toured much of the area and focused their attention on a knoll overlooking the Potomac. Although the origin of the hill's name has been lost to history, the two men decided that the site, Jenkins Hill, was "a pedestal waiting for a monument." That monument was to be the United States Capitol.

With the location of the Capitol established, L'Enfant set about the task of determining the location of the other major structure, the President's Mansion, and a network of roads. His plan for the streets called for the development of a system of highways that would create grand intersections and circles throughout the major areas of the city.

To help provide some guidance and examples of what he wanted to design, L'Enfant requested a number of maps with plans of European cities from Jefferson, who had acquired them while he served as ambassador to France. Of these city maps, the two most influential ones were those of the town of Versailles, famous for its palace and broad avenues, and a detailed layout of central Paris. These maps provided L'Enfant with the needed inspiration for the layout of the Mall and the President's Mansion, and the grand diagonal streets that would be named after each of the states.

The eventual layout and relationship of the Capitol, the President's Mansion, and a proposed monument to George Washington bear a remarkable similarity to the center of L'Enfant's home town, Paris. He arranged these three structures in an L-shaped pattern. The Capitol was to be placed at the end of the tall part of the letter; the monument to Washington would be located at the angle; and the White House would be situated at the end of the short leg of the L.

L'Enfant's plan took into consideration the layout of Paris of that period as well as a number of efforts to redesign some parts of the old city center during the latter part of the 18th century. He was familiar with the layout of three of the most important sites in central Paris that formed an L-shaped pattern. The Palace of the Louvre, seat of the French king while he resided in Paris, was located along the banks of the Seine River. The building's location would correspond to the one proposed for the U.S. Capitol. The site selected for the monument to Washington would relate to the Place de Louis XV, which was located at the angle of the L. This area, now known as the Place de la Concorde, was the spot

For guidance in designing the new city, cosmopolitan world traveler Thomas Jefferson supplied L'Enfant with maps of European cities, which he had obtained while serving as ambassador to France.

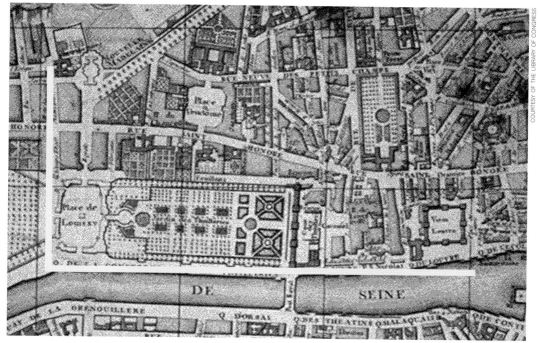

L'Enfant's hometown, Paris, hugs the Seine River. Important buildings —the Louvre, the Place de la Concorde, and the seat of the Bishop of Paris—form a rough L in city center. L'Enfant would remember the layout while designing Washington.

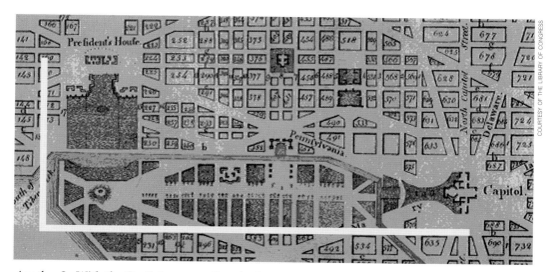

Another L: With the Capitol representing the Louvre, a proposed monument to George Washington at the site of the Place de la Concorde, and the President's House where the Bishop's residence was located, L'Enfant brought a little bit of Paris to Washington.

where members of the French nobility were guillotined during the mid-1790s.

At the other end of the L was the site of a church and seat of the Bishop of Paris since the 13th century. The church that L'Enfant knew was begun in 1757 in the form of a Greek temple and was not completed until 85 years later. Its significance to L'Enfant was that it was situated at the end of the Rue Royale (Royal Road) and connected the Bishop of Paris with the seat of royal power.

Although he was a remarkable individual and creative in his

CONSTITUTIONAL CONGRESS
Federal Hall, New York, New York
March 4, 1789 – August 12, 1790

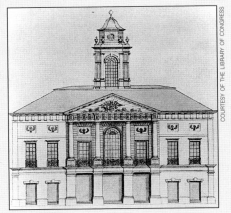

FEDERAL HALL, NEW YORK, NEW YORK

When they moved to New York, members wanted a Capitol befitting Congress' new stature under the Constitution. They chose a building on Wall Street and hired Major Peter (Pierre) Charles L'Enfant to renovate it. Renamed Federal Hall, it became the first structure built or renovated expressly for the purpose of becoming the Capitol of the United States.

During this important period, the Founding Fathers established the processes and governmental institutions so familiar to Americans today. Congress' first job was to count the electoral votes George Washington received and to certify his election as President. Congress also passed, and the states later ratified, the first ten amendments to the Constitution, the Bill of Rights.

Early in the session, Congress concentrated on the establishment of a permanent location for the federal government, as set forth in Article I, section 8 of the Constitution, and local, state, and regional leaders lobbied for various sites. Alexander Hamilton, secretary of the treasury, became

a leader in the debate and settled two major issues through the Compromise of 1790. It called for the North to give up its ambitions for the Capitol and authorized its location along the Potomac River. To get this concession, southern states had to agree that the federal government would accept the North's large Revolutionary War debts. Hamilton's coup achieved his long-standing goal of financially tying the states to the success of the federal government. The final article of the compromise called for the government to move to Philadelphia for ten years before going to the new city on the Potomac by December 1800.

TIME LINE   ☆ *The French Revolution began on July 14, 1789.*

grand designs for the federal city, L'Enfant suffered from several major personality traits that put him at odds wth the commissioners. He was conceited, secretive, and did not work well with others. L'Enfant worked diligently on the plan for the federal city, but he never reconciled himself to the fact that the commissioners were his bosses. George Washington had written to him in no uncertain terms reminding him that even though he had sponsored him, the commissioners were in charge, and he had to report to them and follow their instructions.

The commissioners were businessmen and farmers as well as

CONSTITUTIONAL CONGRESS
Congress Hall,
Philadelphia, Pennsylvania
December 6, 1790 – May 14, 1800

Since Philadelphia was the largest and most cosmopolitan city in the country, many members of Congress looked forward to the move and to the social life and comforts of the city.

In 1791, Hamilton was able to persuade George Washington and Congress to establish a national bank through his interpretation of Article I, section 8 of the Constitution. Thomas Jefferson opposed the move. Known as the elastic clause, the article provides that Congress can "make all Laws which shall be necessary and proper." Jefferson contended that this meant Congress could only pass laws necessary to operate the government—not laws it simply wanted. This marked the beginning of the ongoing struggle for a balance of power between the legislative and the executive branches of government, and the emergence of a two-party political system. While members of Congress

CONGRESS HALL, PHILADELPHIA, PENNSYLVANIA

debated and enjoyed themselves in Philadelphia, George Washington worked diligently to make the new federal city on the Potomac a reality. In 1791, a surveying team began laying out the boundaries of what would become the District of Columbia, and Peter L'Enfant was charged with designing the city and the Capitol. On September 18, 1793, Washington laid the cornerstone for the Capitol.

☆ *In 1793, France's King Louis XVI was beheaded.*

ardent supporters of the new nation. They saw the project as an economic opportunity to sell land and to make more money; L'Enfant envisioned the city in artistic terms. With these two widely divergent views, inevitably the commissioners and L'Enfant would fail to understand each other; and conflict seemed unavoidable.

Several events in the fall of 1791 strained the relationship between the commissioners and L'Enfant to the breaking point. L'Enfant did not want to see the commissioners gain financially by virtue of their position, and refused to provide them with a copy of his plan. As a result, the first two auctions of lots in the city netted only a few sales. Although L'Enfant and the commissioners saw the world differently and had justifiable reasons for what they did, the commissioners were his superiors, and the city needed the money from land sales to help pay for what L'Enfant envisioned.

With an African American holding his horse, L'Enfant shows Washington a plat on Jenkins Hill, site of the future Capitol. The painting, part of a mural, was completed in 1974 in the House Restaurant corridor.

As their vituperative relationship became more strained with each passing day, they communicated less and less with each other. Adding to the growing conflict, L'Enfant and a major landowner, who was a relative of one of the commissioners, became embroiled in a nasty dispute. Daniel Carroll of Duddington, a member of the Carroll family and related to Commissioner Daniel Carroll of Rock Creek, asked L'Enfant to give him information about the city plan so that he would know where he could build a house in the southern part of the city. L'Enfant did not respond to his request. When he did not get an answer after repeated inquiries, Carroll of Duddington selected a site and proceeded to build his home.

A similar episode shortly ensued that involved Notley Young, another influential landowner who also built a home. When L'Enfant discovered that the two houses interfered with his proposed street plan, he tried unsuccessfully to communicate with the two landowners to tell them to stop building at once. Since

L'Enfant received no answer and Carroll's house projected into the middle of his planned New Jersey Avenue, he ordered the house to be "carefully" torn down, and had the bricks placed in neat piles off to the side of the proposed road. Distraught, the Carrolls made the situation known to Washington.

Washington saw L'Enfant as being politically deaf and the commissioners as lacking any concept of Washington and L'Enfant's shared vision for the city. After a flurry of attempts by Washington to point out to the commissioners that L'Enfant was the best qualified person for the job and reminding L'Enfant that he must work with the commissioners, L'Enfant informed Washington that he had had enough.

The temperamental L'Enfant resigned in March 1792, without having completed or published his design for the city. However, just before resigning, he had submitted to Washington an almost completed copy of the plan. With the plan in hand, the commissioners turned to Andrew Ellicott and illustrators he had hired to complete the drawings and prepare them for publication. Ellicott was selected for the project since the commissioners had earlier chosen him and his crew, which briefly included the services of Benjamin Banneker, to survey the city. Ellicott was the most able and best informed person to understand L'Enfant's plan and to bring it to fruition. Many events in this stage of the planning have

Late 18th-century travelers look upon the bucolic site of the future city from Georgetown Heights in Maryland. Today's Roosevelt Island sits midstream in the Potomac River.

become clouded in history and have been a source of a major controversy about the roles Peter L'Enfant, Andrew Ellicott and his brothers, one of whom was named Benjamin, and Benjamin Banneker played in the final layout of the federal city. By 1794, Andrew Ellicott had fallen prey to some of the same problems L'Enfant experienced. Ellicott became embroiled with the commissioners over unjustified discrepancies in the survey as well as other matters, and he was subsequently fired. Such acrimonious personality conflicts became a constant theme in the history of the building of the Capitol.

Benjamin Banneker's Contribution to the New Nation

The life and achievements of Benjamin Banneker are significant in history and important to the aspirations of African Americans during the early years of the republic. During his lifetime, from 1731 until his death in October 1806, Banneker had become recognized in the United States and Europe for his knowledge of mathematics and astronomy, as a writer of almanacs, and for his public stance on slavery and the general condition of Africans living in America. However, with the passage of time, his contributions to the creation of the federal city have become obscured in legend and myth.

To mark a ten-mile-square for the new federal city, workmen planted 40 boundary stones such as this one at one-mile intervals in Maryland and Virginia. Andrew Ellicott and a free black mathematician and astronomer, Benjamin Banneker, marked spots for them by surveying.

Born near Baltimore, Maryland, Banneker had become known throughout central Maryland by the 1760s for his scientific knowledge, for attention to exact details, and for building a clock. He designed and built a clock entirely of wood, which kept almost perfect time in hours and minutes for more than fifty years. One person in particular who had learned of Banneker's abilities was Thomas Jefferson, then secretary of state.

When the three commissioners chose Andrew Ellicott to head the surveying team that was to lay out the ten-square-mile boundary lines of the District, he began to assemble the men needed for the arduous undertaking. The Ellicott family lived just south of Baltimore and also had become aware of Banneker's reputation and abilties.

Ellicott needed someone skilled in using scientific instruments and taking precise astronomical readings. Qualified individuals he had worked with in the past were not available, and as an alternative, his brother, George Ellicott, suggested Banneker. Although Banneker was 60 years old, suffered from arthritis, and lacked any practical surveying experience, he would be able to perform all the scientific duties until a younger person could be found.

Jefferson also had recommended Banneker as an excellent choice for the beginning phase of the project, a survey that took almost two years to complete.

After a long, cold, wet ride in February 1791, Ellicott and Banneker arrived in Arlington, Virginia, where Banneker was fully introduced to his complex and demanding duties. At a starting point near Arlington, the team would go northwest for ten miles, make a right angle turn toward the northeast for ten miles, make another 90° turn to the southeast, go another ten miles, and make a final turn to the southwest for an additional ten miles to complete the square. Banneker would assist Ellicott with the observations, but the most important part of his job was to maintain the clock that Ellicott had made for surveying. The clock needed to be kept wound, celestial sightings had to be performed several times each day to insure the clock's accuracy, and the clock needed to be kept at a constant temperature to reduce the expansion and contraction of the parts in the mechanism. This required Banneker to spend almost all of his time in a cold tent to maintain the instruments, enduring the winter weather while the rest of the crew spent their nights in a local inn.

Banneker was only able to sleep a few hours at any one time because of his almost

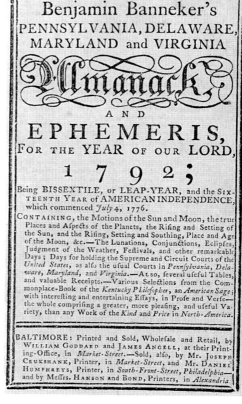

constant duties, and he was not accustomed to living outdoors in harsh conditions. As the weeks passed, his health deteriorated due to the lack of sleep and his arthritis, and he informed Ellicott that he wanted to return to his farm and complete work on his almanac. Although the exact date of his departure is unknown, the historical record indicates that it was sometime in the latter part of April 1791. Banneker returned to his farm, and he was able to publish his almanac the following year. Benjamin Ellicott assumed Banneker's duties of maintaining the instruments for the remainder of the survey.

In the mist of history, Banneker has been given credit for recreating Peter L'Enfant's plan for the federal city after L'Enfant refused to give it to the district commissioners. Some believe that in 1791 Andrew Ellicott and L'Enfant worked together for the district commissioners, but records clearly indicate that each had his own mandate and his own staff. L'Enfant's appointment did not

Benjamin Banneker's Almanack—his first— appeared after he had finished surveying Washington, in 1792. Part of its title: "Being Bissextile, or Leap-Year, and the Sixteenth Year of American Independence." The last issue was published in 1797. The versatile Banneker also computed the cycle of the 17-year locust.

begin until a month after Ellicott and Banneker began work on the survey. Also, Banneker terminated his ties with Ellicott and the commissioners only a few weeks before L'Enfant could even have begun developing his design for the city. However, the professional careers of Andrew Ellicott and L'Enfant did cross in 1792. Because of L'Enfant's intransigence in providing a finished plan, it fell to Ellicott to complete the last few details and small modifications needed in L'Enfant's final proposal submitted to Washington on February 20, 1792. Ellicott subsequently hired two illustrators to put some artistic touches on the map to make it look more appealing to prospective real estate investors. The final version included the combined efforts of L'Enfant, Ellicott, and his artists.

U. S. CAPITOL, WASHINGTON, D. C.

CONSTITUTIONAL CONGRESS
U. S. Capitol, Washington, D. C.
November 17, 1800 – Present

Built on Jenkins Hill overlooking the Potomac River, the U.S. Capitol has a 200-year history of being built, rebuilt, expanded, and restored. During the first several years, Congress, the Supreme Court, and the Library of Congress were housed in the Senate wing, the only completed section of the building when the government moved to its new permnanent home in 1800. The House wing was finished in 1807.

Congress reconvened in the Capitol in 1819 after the British burned it in 1814. By the 1850s, the building went through a major reconstruction, which was completed after the conclusion on the Civil War. Aside from an extension of the east front between 1958 and 1961, the exterior of the Capitol has remained basically unchanged since 1865.

TIME LINE ☆ *In 1801, President John Adams became one of the first leaders in history to peacefully yield power to a political opponent, Thomas Jefferson.*

A New Capitol for a New Nation

1792-1850

Gnome-like figures frolic atop pediments in a Capitol design-contest entry from Philip Hart of Maryland. District commissioners solicited designs for the new building from the public but rejected the dozen or so they received.

DESIGNING A CAPITOL FOR CONGRESS

With Andrew Ellicott's city survey well underway and the contentious relationship with L'Enfant at an end, George Washington, Thomas Jefferson, and the three commissioners turned their attention to building the Capitol. When the commissioners hired L'Enfant, he was subsequently asked not only to design the layout of the city but also to develop plans for the Capitol and the President's Mansion. Whenever the commissioners made inquiries about his ideas for the buildings, he replied, "I have a design in my head." And that was where it remained—if he had ever had one.

Washington faced a deadline. On the first Monday of December 1800, eight short years away, he had to have a place for Congress to meet, a home for the President, and enough of the city completed for the government's scheduled move from Philadelphia. In early 1792, he possessed a city plan on paper, but he had to find someone to produce a design for the Capitol and the President's Mansion to make the plan a reality.

Washington and Jefferson, both experienced in architecture,

decided that a nationwide competition would be the best way to get the finest designs possible for the two buildings. In March 1792, the commissioners placed advertisements in the leading newspapers in all the states and offered an award of a city lot and $500 for the winning design. The deadline for the competition was July 15, 1792. To be eligible for consideration, the design had to include elevations, drawings of the façade, the types and amounts of bricks and stones to be used, and cross-sections of the building to illustrate the foundation and structural elements, such as columns, arches, porches, and roof design.

Physician, painter, and inventor, William Thornton turned amateur architect to design the U. S. Capitol. Born on a tiny island near Tortola in the West Indies, he had moved to the U. S. in 1787.

More than a dozen plans were submitted, but none met with approval. America then did not have many professional architects, which became painfully apparent when Washington, Jefferson, and the commissioners reviewed the submissions. One set of Capitol drawings showed four columns in the central areas of each of the rooms designed for the House of Representatives, the Senate, and the Supreme Court Chambers. This proposal would have created so many visual barriers in each room that public debates in the chambers would have been impossible. Another entry failed to use proper perspectives, looked amateurish in its overall design, and lacked any information concerning door and window details, steps, and porches.

Two designs submitted by Marylanders included bizarre creatures perched on the building. One showed a very large, fantastical looking bird on top of the Dome. It resembled a huge rooster ready to take flight, or perhaps a phoenix rising from the ashes. The other plan called for the placement of humanoid figures around the top of the façade. The gnome-like creatures were dressed only in loincloths and seemed to be waving spears that pointed in various directions, and two of them appeared to be in a position to play golf.

Although no record exists of Washington's or Jefferson's personal reactions to some of the entries, they did receive one plan that showed promise. Stephen Hallet, who was born in France and moved to Philadelphia in the late 1780s, had developed a model based on neo-classical architecture, but it included a number of features exhibiting a strong French influence. Even though the plan held promise, the "fancy piece" design, as Jefferson referred to it, failed to meet a number of the necessary criteria of the competition. By late summer 1792, the commissioners had decided to ask Hallet to produce another version based on their suggested corrections and to make the plan more economical. He began to redo his design, believing that he had won the contest and that he only needed to make some technical modifications.

Meanwhile, another contestant, William Thornton, had contacted the commissioners and asked for an extension of the deadline in order to complete his design. Since they had not received a completely satisfactory plan, they agreed to the extension, but only for the Capitol building since James Hoban's design for the President's Mansion had already been accepted. After a number of exchanges, Thornton finally submitted his sketches to

Prize-winning design by Thornton featured two wings and a low

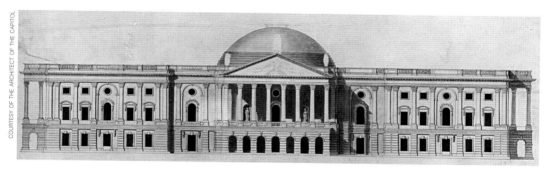

COURTESY OF THE ARCHITECT OF THE CAPITOL

Washington in January 1793. He passed them on to Jefferson and the commissioners with the comment, "The Grandeur, Simplicity, and Beauty of the exterior—the propriety with which the apartments are distributed—and the economy in the mass of the whole structure, will I doubt not give it a preference in your eyes, as it has done in mine." Jefferson made similar remarks of praise, and in March, the commissioners gave the prize to Thornton.

Sensing that they had been unfair to Hallet and because questions had been raised about the interior spaces in Thornton's plan, Washington suggested to the commissioners that they compensate Hallet to placate him. In an agreement that they later regretted, they offered Hallet the cash equivalent to Thornton's prize of $500 and a city lot—plus the authority to supervise the completion of Thornton's plan. Hallet resented Thornton and eagerly called attention to a number of interior design problems. Since none of Thornton's original drawings exist, it is impossible to know the validity of Hallet's comments or whether he was simply making mischief to get revenge. He happily pointed out that the floor plan of the building was not structurally sound and that some of the rooms would not have enough light. Undoubtedly, the Rotunda in Thornton's design would have been a very dark place since there were no large windows or skylights in the room. The only light would have come from candles, an open door, and one small, round window.

After a committee comprised of Thornton, Hallet, James Hoban, Thomas Jefferson, and two others met to resolve the design deficiencies in Thornton's plan during 1793, the commis-

dome. This drawing from the late 1790s replaces his original, which has been lost. His design "captivated the eyes and judgment of all," said Thomas Jefferson, and Washington praised the design for its "Grandeur, Simplicity and Convenience." Thornton's prize: $500 and a city lot.

sioners created more conflict by placing Hallet in charge of construction of the Capitol. He proceeded to make unauthorized changes in Thornton's design and failed to follow instructions issued by the commissioners. Hallet's actions eventually led to reprimands and a final break with the commissioners on November 15, 1794. However, before discharging him, the commissioners had placed Hallet under the direction of James Hoban, who now had to oversee the completion of the President's Mansion and also undo Hallet's unauthorized alterations to the Capitol.

THE CORNERSTONE: A CAPITOL MYSTERY

Dressed in Masonic aprons, sashes, and collars, George Washington and fellow Masons gather to lay the cornerstone of the new Capitol. At the September 18, 1793 event, bands played and spectators cheered. But no one marked the exact location of the cornerstone, so its precise whereabouts remain a mystery.

The controversy among Thornton, Hallet, and the commissioners came at a time when George Washington desperately wanted to get the Capitol construction underway. After having forced the feuding architects to resolve their differences, he then set the date of September 18, 1793, for the laying of the cornerstone. The *Alexandria Gazette* provided the only surviving firsthand account of the ceremony and events leading up to it. Amid great fanfare, Washington led a parade from Georgetown to Capitol Hill, with flags flying, bands playing, and jubilant spectators cheering. The distance could be covered today in about an hour on foot but those making the trek that day did not have paved streets and bridges. The *Gazette* referred to Pennsylvania Avenue, which connects the President's Mansion and the Capitol, as a bog, and the marchers were forced to go by a longer and less traveled route. Nearing Capitol Hill, the procession had to cross Tiber Creek, which today is buried under Constitution Avenue. In 1793 few bridges existed, and many observers had to wade across the stream as the bands and artillery crossed on a small, wooden bridge.

Once everyone had arrived, George Washington began the ceremony. The laying of the cornerstone was a solemn event that followed ancient Masonic rituals. Masons described themselves as a brotherhood that believed in a deity, service to better mankind, and education. Washington, who had been the Grand Master of the Alexandria Lodge, led its members and others from Maryland lodges in the ceremony. The entourage came dressed in Masonic aprons, sashes, and collars, and presented the symbolic gifts of corn, representing goodness and plenty; wine, embodying refreshment and health; and oil, a symbol of joy and gladness. Before laying the stone, Washington spread mortar on the bed stone and carefully laid a silver plate on it. The cornerstone was then placed on top of the plate. The plate bore the inscription:

> *This South East corner Stone, of the Capitol of the United States of America in the City of Washington, was laid on the 18th day of September, in the thirteenth year of American Independence, in the first year of the second term of the Presidency of George Washington.*

The inscription concluded with the names of the three city commissioners. Once the stone was in place, the proceedings ended with a prayer, Masonic chants, and a series of fifteen short orations punctuated by volley salutes from the artillery.

After the ceremony, the crowd joined Washington in a feast on Jenkins Hill that included a 500-pound barbequed ox. All the participants had what was called "Potomac Fever"—a term applied to those who strongly supported the establishment of the federal city along the banks of the Potomac—and they were elated that the Capitol was now turning into a reality.

In their excitement, however, no one remembered to mark for

Early drawing shows the Senate wing completed but the House wing still a ghostly sketch. The Senate, House, and the Supreme Court all used this boxlike structure, first of the Capitol's components to be completed.

posterity the site of the cornerstone. To this day, the location of the stone remains a mystery, and all efforts to find it have failed. Historians have argued that since Masonic rules require a cornerstone to be laid at the southeast corner of a building, and the *Alexandria Gazette* clearly stated that was where the ceremony took place, the stone should be in the southeast corner of the Capitol.

But where was the southeast corner of the Capitol in 1793? The only section of the Capitol completed during the initial building phase was the Senate wing, which was opened in November 1800. It has long been believed that the cornerstone was in the corner of

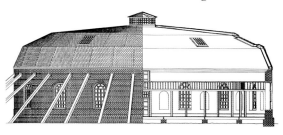

Timbers support the poorly constructed walls of the "Oven,"

a temporary brick structure that accommodated the House of Representatives. It was built in 1800 and razed in 1804.

that building, and in 1893, a group of Washington, D.C., citizens placed a plaque there, commemorating the 100th anniversary of the laying of the cornerstone. However, in 1959, when construction crews excavated around the original east front of the Capitol, preparing to add a 32–foot extension to the central façade, a search for the cornerstone ended in failure. Additional attempts in the early 1980s and another in the late 1980s using ground-penetrating radar also ended in disappointment. Before the century ended, the Army Corps of Engineers made still another attempt but failed to find it or any silver residue, which should have been present, even if the plate had oxidized.

Some historians have argued that since the initial construction of the building included the foundations for the House wing and the Rotunda, the silver plate would be in the southeast corner of the House's portion of the Capital. Building records indicate that during the initial construction period, from 1793 until 1796, excavators had begun work on all three areas—the Senate wing, the House wing, and the Rotunda—and that foundation and stone work had progressed to some extent throughout the entire site. However, that came to an end in August 1796 when all work ceased except on the Senate wing. By then it had become clear that, given the available labor force, the entire Capitol could not be finished in time for the 1800 move of Congress from Philadelphia. In addition, the federal government lacked the funds to finish the work. As a result, from 1796 until 1800, all efforts and resources went into completing just the Senate wing.

In 1993, an attempt was made to locate the cornerstone and silver plate in the southeast corner of the old House wing. After carefully excavating the area, crews found what they believed to be the cornerstone and performed another ground penetrating radar scan. They detected metal, but it turned out to be shims used to level stones. Like the area around the corner of the Senate wing, this site was the scene of major work in 1959 during the east front expansion project, and the shims dated from that period.

So where are the cornerstone and the silver plate? Only the discovery of the plate would absolutely confirm the stone's location. Failure to find the plate continues to raise questions about where it is or what happened to it. The *Alexandria Gazette* reported that "three most Worshipful Masters, descended to the Cavesson trench and deposed the plate, and laid on it the Corner Stone of the Capitol of the United States." This article clearly states that the stone was placed on top of the plate, so it would be highly unlikely, if not impossible, for someone to remove it later and keep it for a trophy. On the other hand, if the plate were still under a stone in either the Senate or House wings, scientists should have detected it with radar or found some silver residue in the area around the foundation.

At least two other possibilities exist concerning the plate's location: The cornerstone was not laid at either of the two sites investigated and is in some other area, or the plate was removed at some other time. The most likely period for the removal would have been between 1801, when the "Oven," a temporary structure where the House of Representatives met, was built, and 1804, when it was razed to make way for the new House wings. Still, the mystery surrounding Washington's silver plate remains a source of endless speculation—and of frustration for those who search for it.

AFRICAN AMERICANS AND THE LIFE OF THE CITY

Shackled slaves trudge down a Washington street. With skilled labor in short supply, many slaves were hired out to work as laborers, carpenters, bricklayers, and stone carvers on the Capitol. The money they earned—some $5 a month—went to their owners.

In the early years of the nation, African Americans played an important role in the construction of the Capitol as well as in the life of the new city. Generally, the historical record does not cover free blacks and slaves as fully as it does for national and state officials, but many references and records about them exist in the National Archives, in state and city historical societies, and in personal papers. Pay vouchers, one of the best sources of information, show that the architect of the President's House, James Hoban, rented some of his slaves during its construction. Other prominent slaveowners related to the commissioners leased their slaves for the building of the Capitol. Since skilled labor was in short supply in the region and many African Americans had been taught a wide variety of professional trades, it was inevitable that they would be hired out by their owners. Over the years, a more complete historical picture has emerged, revealing a glimpse of the African American experience in the new capital.

Soon after Benjamin Banneker had made his contribution to the survey of the city, Peter L'Enfant leased slaves from local Maryland and Virginia owners to assist him in laying out the area where the Capitol and the President's Mansion would be located. In 1791, with the permission of the commissioners, L'Enfant purchased a stone quarry at the mouth of Aquia Creek, approximately 40 miles south in central Virginia, containing a fine grade of sandstone that would be used to face the President's House and the Capitol. A Scottish mason took control of the operation at the quarry the following year and used a large number of slaves to cut and shape stones before they were shipped up the Potomac on flat-bottomed boats.

Once the stone arrived at the docks along the Anacostia River, it was hauled by horse-drawn wagons up to Capitol Hill where work on the foundation was underway. Slaves, European-American laborers, and skilled masons all worked together to ready the foundation for George Washington's laying of the cornerstone. As the building progressed, records indicate that during the winter of 1794-1795, 60 individuals were on the payroll, including four African Americans and one overseer. Between 1795 and the completion of the Senate wing in 1800, a total of 122 African American "hires" were employed as manual laborers, carpenters, bricklayers, and stone carvers on the Hill.

Life was hard in the construction camp. Most slaves lived in shacks, each earning as much as five dollars per month for their masters. The owners dispensed a very small percentage of that to their slaves for their housing and incidentals, which all too often meant liquor. To help ease the situation for the crew of laborers and slaves assigned to make bricks during the winter of 1796-1797, the commissioners provided a couple of hundred barrels of meat and hundreds of barrels of corn-meal to supplement their diets. During the following year, the carpenters were instructed to keep all the scrap lumber for the free laborers and slaves to use for firewood during the coming winter.

Even though Congress moved into the Capitol during November 1800, work on the building was far from complete. By 1814, the House wing had been finished, and a causeway connected the two wings. However, in August, during the War of 1812, British troops under the command of Admiral Sir George Cockburn invaded Washington and burned all public buildings, including the Capitol and the President's House.

After the fire in 1814, slaves made a large contribution in the rebuilding of the Capitol's damaged wings and in the completion of the Rotunda in the 1820s. Because much of the stone in the Capitol had been damaged, Charles Bulfinch, then the new architect, wanted the work completed in marble, which was much better than sandstone but which was also much more expensive to cut and finish. After long debates between Congress and the commissioners about the spiraling costs and the problems of completing the building, government officials took control of the marble quarry in Maryland near the Potomac River and ran it with federal funds. After the government officials took charge, they found that they had to house and feed the labor force of both free men and slaves. Labor costs kept escalating, and by 1818, laborers were being paid up to $1 a day, and skilled stone cutters were earning more than twice that much.

Even after the Capitol was completed, the issues of slaves, slavery, and African Americans in the city remained matters of con-

Somber cabinet secretaries listen as President Abraham Lincoln offers the "First Reading of the Emancipation Proclamation" in an 1864 painting by Francis B. Carpenter.

cern on the Hill. In 1827, aside from all the well-known congressional debates about slavery, the city placed a number of civil rights restrictions, including a curfew, on all African Americans. During the following year, Congress had all African Americans blocked from entering the Capitol unless they were on official business or were hired to maintain the building. However, things improved during the Civil War. Congress freed all the slaves in the city in April 1862 and compensated their owners up to $300 per slave for the loss of their property, the only instance in which the government paid for the freeing of slaves. Shortly after the emancipation order, most of the civil restrictions on African Americans were removed, and they were granted many of the freedoms enjoyed by other residents of the city.

MOVING TO THE NEW FEDERAL CITY

On July 16, 1790, Congress had agreed to the Compromise of 1790 providing for the government to move from Philadelphia to the new federal city in ten years, a move that many members and executive department bureaucrats did not welcome. In the late 18th century, Philadelphia's population exceeded 40,000 citizens. Its population was generally well educated, the city contained a thriving business community, and its social life was without par in America. A large percentage of the people lived in well-built homes, many of brick, and the city had a number of paved streets. For those members and officials from the northern states, Philadelphia possessed another appealing quality: Through the influence of the large Quaker congregations, the state, in 1780, had adopted a scheme for the gradual abolition of slavery.

Philadelphia possessed all the dignity and charm of a great city, and the impending move to the new capital on the Potomac was a daunting and distressing prospect. What roads had been built between the two cities were little more than dirt trails into the wilderness. Few taverns existed beyond Baltimore, Maryland, or Lancaster, Pennsylvania, and those members accustomed to the finery of Philadelphia considered them no more than hovels. The fare included poorly cooked food and locally prepared beverages, not the fine wines of Philadelphia, and sleeping accommodations often required sharing rooms and sometimes even beds with other travelers.

Those who wanted to travel by water could book passage on a small boat, sail down the Delaware River, out into the Atlantic, into the Chesapeake Bay, and up the Potomac River. However, seafaring was not without its problems. Accommodations were cramped, loading and unloading of baggage took time, and ships would, all too frequently, take on water and sometimes sink.

Weather presented another problem in the Middle Atlantic, where hurricanes could suddenly occur during the late summer and fall.

The "Removal," the term used at the time for the move, began in March 1800 and continued through the winter of 1801. Many executive branch offices, such as the departments of Treasury, and State and the office of the Postmaster General, along with the support staff for Congress—officers, clerks, and doorkeepers—came early. The initial move took place while Congress was in recess, allowing the 100 to 150 members of the support staff and government bureaucrats to set up their offices and to find some place to live before Congress opened for business. A few government employees simply resigned their posts rather than face the prospect of moving to the "wilderness." However, many perceived the move as a final tribute to George Washington, who had died in December 1799. They also looked forward to escaping the all too frequent yellow fever epidemics in Philadelphia.

The relocation required transporting everything the government owned and would need in its new home. All the official records, including tax rolls, patents, letters, reports, books, the Declaration of Independence, and the Constitution of the United States, would have to be packed and protected for the wagon trip from Philadelphia. Officials had decided to send these irreplaceable documents overland rather than to risk shipping them by water. However, desks, chairs, bookcases, cabinets, quills and ink, candles, and almost every replaceable item the government needed went by ship. Family members had to go through the moving process as well, and for those well-to-do government employees, household servants and slaves became part of the entourage headed for Washington.

Packing and moving proved slow and difficult. Everything had to be carefully loaded and secured for protection against the weather. Travel overland by wagon took from three to ten days, depending on conditions, and some men became so ill from the rigors of the journey that they had to rest at local taverns until their health returned. The process of packing, loading, and unloading for the passage by boat proved equally difficult and time consuming since everything first had to be loaded onto wagons and then taken to the pier for loading aboard ship. The process had to be repeated in reverse when the boats arrived in

Rustic Suter's Tavern in Georgetown welcomed travelers to and from the Capitol. George Washington met here with major landowners along the Potomac River to discuss plans for the new city.

Washington. The experience, however, was not total drudgery for one group of State Department workers. One day, a supervisor decided to treat his staff to a supply of beer. Apparently that turned out to be such a hit with his men that the following day he provided another round of beer, this time supplemented with liquors, no doubt lightening everyone's task preparing for the long journey through Pennsylvania and Maryland.

By 1800, the wilderness called the City of Washington, named by the commissioners in September 1791 to honor George Washington, consisted of approximately 100 brick homes, less than 300 wood dwellings, a few brick buildings for departments of the executive branch, an unfinished President's Mansion, and

Taking shape, the new federal city sprawls across the rolling hills of the District of Columbia. A broad new boulevard—Pennsylvania Avenue—stretches from Capitol Hill to the distant President's Mansion.

one wing of the proposed Capitol. Government officials, upon their arrival, were greeted with a vista of a city in name only.

One lady referred to Washington as "a city of streets without houses." The unfinished Capitol stood on top of Jenkins Hill, and two miles away, workers busily endeavored to complete the President's Mansion. To travel from the President's Mansion to Capitol Hill, one had to brave the unfinished roads that L'Enfant had laid out. A city resident described Pennsylvania Avenue connecting the President's Mansion and the Capitol, "as a deep morass covered with stumps and alder bushes." New Jersey Avenue, where L'Enfant and Daniel Carroll came to such an impasse, had only two buildings along its entire length. Abbé Correa de Serra, a Portuguese diplomat and a friend of Thomas Jefferson, portrayed the new capital as a "city of Magnificent Distances." With its 100-square-mile area, the city even surpassed the size of London in 1800.

The size of the government workforce in 1800 pales in comparison with that of today, but even the small number of employees placed a strain on the housing market. With so few facilities to buy or rent, the market forces caused prices in Washington to rise to twice those paid in Philadelphia. In the early 1800s, a private room in Washington City could cost approximately $11 per week; one with double occupancy could rent for about a dollar less for each person. Members of Congress and their staff tried to find suitable accommodations near the Capitol, and executive branch workers sought places around the President's Mansion. Some, who desired more elegant living and could afford higher rates, moved to the well-established and wealthier Georgetown, which meant a long, four-mile ride to the Capitol or a little shorter one to work for the President.

Abigail Adams, wife of President John Adams and the first presidential spouse to live in the White House, found it appallingly unfinished.

First Lady Abigail Adams, who moved from her comfortable surroundings in Massachusetts, was loath to find her new home encircled by stacks of bricks, workers' sheds, and piles of construction debris. To her horror, the inside of the President's House had none of the allure of a mansion but all the aura of living in a damp, noisy, and dirty construction site. Plasterers had not finished the walls, and the dampness and smell of the wet plaster permeated the house. She soon found that no practical laundry service existed, and she had to make use of what is known today as the East Room to hang her laundry. To dry the clothing, she took advantage of the fireplaces in the room, which the plasterers kept stoked all day to help dry the plaster before the onset of winter.

While the Adams family lived in only a shell of a house, it at least was a full-size shell with most of the major work finished. The Capitol, however, stood with only a third of the building completed. It proved difficult to get skilled workers to move to Washington because they had to leave well-established jobs elsewhere and compete with the wages paid for slave labor. The only other available skilled workers were Europeans, mainly Scottish, and they were all too often a cantankerous lot. By 1796, work had ceased on the House wing and Rotunda due to a lack of money and a shortage of skilled labor.

Of the East Room, she wrote, "I make a drying-room of, to hang up the clothes in." Builder and designer of the White House James Hoban also supervised construction at the Capitol.

Meanwhile, America's relations with France deteriorated. The French, who were at war with Britain, became increasingly hostile toward the United States for refusing to support France in the conflict. France began seizing cargo from American ships, bringing on an undeclared naval war that placed a major demand on the treasury's limited funds for a "blue water navy." During an exchange of diplomatic proposals that became known as the XYZ Affair, French Foreign Minister Talleyrand demanded a quarter-million-dollar bribe to accept an American diplomatic delegation. Insulted, Congress resoundingly rejected his ultimatum.

The Capitol in 1800: Here President John Adams addressed the first Joint Session of Congress on November 22. "I congratulate the people of the United States on the assembling of Congress at the permanent seat of their government..." he said. "May this Territory be the residence of virtue and happiness."

Widespread indignation inspired America's well-known response to Talleyrand: "Millions for defense, but not one cent for tribute." Diplomatic negotiations finally ended the dispute.

As a result of the financial drain on the treasury, all efforts focused on completing just the Senate wing before the December 1800 deadline. The sandstone exterior of the building followed Thornton's original design on the east, north, and west façades. The south side was made of brick since it would eventually be joined to the Rotunda. Even though it was only partially completed and looked rather peculiar sitting on top of the hill, the Capitol was still imposing and one of the largest buildings in the Americas. The interior spaces were nearly ready by the end of 1799, and only the finishing touches and some repair of damage caused by winter weather remained to be done before the congressional staff arrived.

The officials and staff who moved into the Capitol included 106 representatives and two delegates from the Northwest Territory, 32 senators, the United States Supreme Court, the Library of Congress, clerks, librarians, and a whole range of support staff to meet congressional needs and to service the building. The senators had the grandest space in the Capitol, a semicircular two-story room that looked out the east front of the building. Besides the Senate Chamber, the first floor consisted of four committee rooms, two entrances, a lobby, and a staircase to the second floor.

The second floor included the Senate gallery, the Library of Congress, one committee room, and offices for the clerk of the House and the Secretary of the Senate. Since the architects had dedicated such a relatively large space to the library and because its collection was so small at the time, the House of Representatives met in the Library of Congress room beginning in November 1800. The members found the space too small, and almost exactly one year later, the representatives moved into the Oven.

Like the House, the Supreme Court spent the first ten years of its tenure in the Capitol without a proper and permanent area dedicated to its needs. Usually the Court met in one of the committee rooms on the first floor, but it would occasionally have to move to another chamber when a House or Senate committee needed the space. On other occasions, the Court, like the House, met in the Library of Congress on the second floor. Fortunately, since the rooms were small, only six justices sat on the Court from 1789 until 1807, when Jefferson proposed and Congress agreed to increase the number of justices to seven.

Even as they strived to complete the Senate wing by the December 1800 deadline, the builders had not neglected an important facility for the new home of Congress. During October, workers installed a 70-foot-long privy for the use of the members at a cost to taxpayers of $234.

Even before Congress, the President, and the executive branch officers completed their move, the city began to feel growing pains from other segments of the population. Office seekers came looking for government jobs, and lobbyists arrived, hoping to influence legislation. The new city's changing population, now with its share of prostitutes and those who subsisted in the drinking houses, created an environment for criminal and other antisocial behavior.

SOCIAL JUSTICE AND PUBLIC MORES IN EARLY WASHINGTON, D.C.

According to Christian Hines's account of early Washington history that was published in 1866, the first public execution in the city occurred during Thomas Jefferson's presidency. Hines, a young man who settled in the new federal city in 1800, witnessed the execution of a murderer within a year or two of his arrival. The execution took place in front of the west side of the Capitol. The gallows was located in the general vicinity of the present reflecting pool and near the statue of General Ulysses S. Grant.

The condemned was a man named McGirk, a bricklayer who frequently patronized local saloons. He came home one evening in a drunken stupor and beat his pregnant wife who suffered a miscarriage of twins and died a short time later.

After a jury found McGirk guilty of murder, he was sentenced to be hanged. As soon as the hangman placed the noose around his neck on the day of the execution, McGirk, apparently feeling an extreme sense of guilt, jumped off the gallows in an attempt to take his own life. Spectators grabbed him and pulled him back onto the platform, but he jumped again. The second leap probably broke his neck and crushed his larynx, killing him.

Soon after McGirk's body had been cut down and placed in a coffin, some local residents came forward and cut off pieces of the execution rope, believing, as many Americans did at the time, that the rope from a hanging would cure such things as headaches and toothaches. Presumably, they preferred this to going to a doctor to be bled or having a dentist pull a tooth without administering anesthesia.

Even in death, McGirk continued to cause problems. He was buried in a graveyard north of the city, beyond what is now Florida Avenue. Friends and relatives of others buried in the cemetery objected so violently to having McGirk there that a delegation dug up his coffin and reburied it in a gully across the road. When McGirk's friends learned what had happened, they moved him back to the cemetery. As soon as they left, the earlier group dug him up a third time and buried him in a swampy area by a creek overgrown with thorn bushes. Several years later, someone installing a fence discovered the coffin while digging a posthole, apparently leaving McGirk with only a fencepost to mark his grave.

Officials conducted subsequent executions further away from the Capitol. The second person hanged was an African American accused of "taking liberties" with a white woman. Typical of the period, racism played a major part in his trial and in the public's attitude toward his alleged crime. Rumors spread throughout the city about a lynching, but vigilantism was held in abeyance, and by court order, the condemned man was executed at a site near the city hall, then located on Pennsylvania Avenue, approximately six blocks west of the unfinished Capitol.

Members of Congress were not immune to committing their own transgressions. Life in Washington during the winter congressional sessions was bleak and lonely unless one could find some form of diversion. Wives and families most often stayed home, leaving members alone in the city. They often lived in boarding houses operated by widows, and shared rooms with other members, government staff, or office seekers. To relieve the monotony of the evenings and weekends, some had the opportunity to go to the theater, occasionally to visit the home of a prominent Washingtonian for tea in the drawing room, or to gamble the evening away playing popular card games. At other times, some members sought the company of the fairer sex.

Most members of Congress led respectable lives in Washington, but a few engaged in some rather tawdry behavior. In one particular instance in 1818, members of a congressional committee found the door to their committee room unexpectedly locked. After they banged on the door and threatened to break it down, the door slowly opened. A young girl who had been selling apples around Capitol Hill came out carrying her basket of fruit, no doubt looking embarrassed. As soon as she left, a red-faced senator came to the door, holding an apple.

On another occasion, a prominent female member of the community suggested to Congress that members had an obligation to the community to provide funds to support the Washington Orphan Asylum. She contended that several dozen women had been left expectant mothers after a particularly long winter session. Congress would not have earmarked funds solely for the orphanage, but it did have the obligation of overseeing the welfare of the city and its citizens.

THE CAPITOL TAKES ANOTHER STEP TOWARD COMPLETION

Soon after Congress first met in Washington, members and other officials complained about their accommodations in the unfinished Capitol and demanded their own chambers as soon as possible. Many representatives undoubtedly resented having to meet in the Senate wing. In addition, they had to deal with the harsh afternoon sun beaming in through the eight large windows along the west side of the building, making it all but impossible to look toward the Speaker's chair without squinting.

In an effort to move the Capitol's south wing toward completion and to meet the needs of the representatives, Jefferson authorized James Hoban to develop several approaches. Hoban offered three choices: Complete the entire wing as planned; construct a temporary wooden building; or erect some type of masonry structure over the central foundation that could become part of the projected finished wing. Because of the huge cost involved in constructing the wing, and with limited funds available, Jefferson quickly dismissed the first idea. He rejected the second proposal because putting up a building that would be torn down in a few years was a waste of money. Jefferson approved the final concept of building a brick structure utilizing some of the central foundation of the south wing. This temporary home of the House became known as the Oven.

Although the building was somewhat round, or oval, one of Jefferson's favorite architectural forms, the Oven was hideous looking and was exceedingly uncomfortable. Completed in 1801, the exterior was constructed of unadorned brick with approximately a dozen or so windows, a larger version of the kind then commonly found in private homes. The roof was composed of a series of flat panels that formed a type of dome but lacking the

With workmen scarce and the Treasury depleted, the government in 1795 and 1796 concentrated on completing the Senate wing. Here it dominates its hill overlooking the city.

Low wooden causeway connects the elegant Senate to the Oven, a structure built over the central foundation and originally intended to be part of the finished House wing.

grace of smooth, curved lines. The new building was connected to the Senate wing by an enclosed wooden causeway that included several water closets, or privies. Detracting further from the appearance of the Capitol, the Oven was so poorly constructed that exterior braces had to be added to it two years later to prevent the roof from pushing the walls out and collapsing the building.

Members and guests in the gallery must have found conditions in the Oven almost intolerable, considering the hygienic practices of the early 19th century. Many members stayed in boarding houses, without regular access to bath and laundry facilities; the privies were nearby in the causeway; and possibly 200 members and guests could be in the room at any given time without adequate air circulation. During the first winter, members began to complain about the poor ventilation, foretelling the conditions they would endure when the weather turned warmer. No doubt it was almost unbearable for visitors to watch and listen to debates from the raised gallery where the stale air accumulated.

All efforts to alleviate the hot, stale atmosphere failed, including adding a cupola to the top of the roof. Fortunately, by 1804 the federal government's financial condition improved, and the political leadership pushed Thornton's design for the Capitol forward. As workers razed the Oven and began construction of the originally proposed House wing, the House of Representatives moved back into the library until its new home was competed in 1807.

In 1803, B. Henry Latrobe, with Jefferson's approval, became

the architect to oversee the construction of the House wing. The President knew Latrobe well and could make sure he remained faithful to Thornton's design. Jefferson also assigned Latrobe the responsibility of refurbishing the Senate wing, which suffered from poor construction and deficient design. Roof leaks, for example, had badly damaged the walls and caused a number of timbers to rot.

Classically elegant, the House Chamber takes form in an architectural drawing by B. Henry Latrobe,

Jefferson had very definite ideas about the design of the House Chamber, ideas that were at odds with those of his new architect. Latrobe wanted to build a semicircular chamber; Jefferson wanted an oval room with many skylights, which Latrobe predicted would leak. The two divergent design concepts and the wills of these two opinionated men became just one more chapter in the ongoing friction among those responsible for building the Capitol.

Jefferson, however, had a great deal of respect for Latrobe and his work. Born and trained as an architect in England, Latrobe had distinguished himself as an architect in Jefferson's eyes as one of the leading advocates of Greek Revival architecture in the United States, a style which gained widespread acceptance in all forms of building in early 19th century America. Before he came to the nation's capital, Latrobe's premiere work in this style had been the Bank of Pennsylvania in Philadelphia, which included Greek columns and a pediment over the entrance. Some, like William Thornton, saw it as a shameful copy of classical architecture, but Jefferson was enamored with the design since he had based his 1785 plan for of the Virginia state capitol on ancient Greek architecture.

Soon after his arrival in Washington in 1803, Latrobe made

appointed architect of the Capitol by Jefferson in 1803. The chamber replaced the hated Oven. "I declared on many and all occasions, Jefferson wrote Latrobe, "that I considered you as the only person in the United Sates who could have executed the... chamber."

several important contributions to the Capitol. While grudgingly following Jefferson's directives, he spent the next eight years completing the House wing, conforming it to Thornton's original plan. By 1807, Latrobe had finished the new oval-shaped Hall of the House of Representatives where members met from 1807 until 1814. All the while, Latrobe had chaffed under Jefferson's refusal to relent on the issue of the semicircular chamber for the House, but he had dutifully followed orders only to be criticized in the end for the room's poor acoustics. Representative John Randolph of Virginia stated bluntly that, acoustically, the chamber was "fit for anything but the use intended."

In spite of the poor acoustics, most members were delighted to finally get into their own, beautiful chamber. The Hall of the House, with its oval-shaped area, was much like the Oven, but without its ventilation problems. To add a touch of grandeur, Latrobe included a row of Corinthian columns around the room. When completed, the House and Senate Chambers had many elegant appointments and beautiful domed ceilings. The House had the skylights Jefferson had demanded to increase the amount of light in the chamber, but, just as Latrobe had predicted, they leaked. In his effort to create these grand spaces for Congress, Latrobe had been accused of becoming more and more extravagant in his selection of materials and ornate design elements, no matter how well justified they were. The issue became an ever-increasing source of friction between Latrobe and his supervisors.

One of the most noteworthy architectural details planned by Latrobe was a set of columns on the first floor of the Senate foyer. In 1809, as part of the system to support the staircase to the second level, he created six unique columns and capitals specifically American. He ordered the stonecutters to make the columns look like cornstalks with open ears of corn forming the capitals. In 1816, Latrobe used another decidedly American theme for columns supporting the small Senate Rotunda that would connect the proposed center section of the Capitol and the Senate Chamber. To the surprise of many of today's visitors and to the chagrin of others, the capitals were decorated with the leaves and flowers of the tobacco plant. In the 1850s, when tobacco was still an accepted and important financial agricultural product, artists and stone cutters working in the Hall of Columns on the ground floor of the new House wing repeated the tobacco leaf motif, substituting thistle for Latrobe's flower.

DEATH COMES TO THE CAPITOL, AND THORNTON'S ROLE ENDS

Many considered Latrobe to be one of the great architects of the time for his work on the Senate and House wings of the Capitol. Others criticized him for extravagant architectural embellishments, the expensive practice of using stone columns instead of the cheaper and more easily constructed brick columns covered with plaster, and for the poor acoustics in the Hall of the House. However, admirers and critics alike agreed that Latrobe could not seem to master one essential building technique: He had trouble consistently building arches that would not collapse.

William Thornton, who did not seem to get along with anybody who challenged his plan of the Capitol, constantly ridiculed Latrobe's work, especially the shortcomings of his arches. During this period, Latrobe worked on numerous projects from Pennsylvania to Virginia, as well as on those in Washington. When he was away, he left John Lenthal to oversee construction projects at the Capitol. Latrobe had complete confidence in Lenthal's knowledge as a building supervisor, and appointed him to the position of clerk of the works. The two men communicated frequently by mail, and in one letter to Lenthal, Latrobe somewhat cavalierly acknowledged his problem with the building of arches: "I have had these accidents before on a larger scale, and must therefore grin and bear it."

Latrobe's nemesis finally led to tragic consequences during the summer of 1808. While Latrobe was on one of his frequent absences from the Capitol, Lenthal wrote him that one of the Senate wing staircases supported by an arch was failing and he feared it might collapse. Latrobe responded to Lenthal's request for help by telling him that he had no idea why the staircase had shifted and was in such an imminent state of failure. Dumfounded, he could not offer any suggestions for a possible solution. He concluded by saying, in effect, that he wanted to "sleep on it," and if he had any ideas, he would write him again.

At this same time, Lenthal and the masons were engaged in building a second and even more important set of arches that Latrobe designed for the Senate and Supreme Court Chambers. One set would support the floor of the Senate Chamber and form the ceiling of the new home of the Supreme Court on the ground floor. Another set would create the ceiling for the Senate Chamber, which was directly above the Court, and reached two stories in height. Latrobe successfully designed the arched ceiling in the Senate Chamber, which proved to be much less of a challenge because it was a two-story semicircular room with a very sharp angle where the vaults intersected with the wall.

The Supreme Court Chamber posed a much greater architectural challenge. The size of the floor space almost equaled that of the Senate Chamber directly above it, but the ceiling was only one story high. This meant that the vaulting would intersect at almost a right angle and that the vaulting would have to carry the weight of the Senate Chamber's floor. The Senate's ceiling only

To honor New World products, Indian-corn sprouts from the top of a column in the original Senate wing. Latrobe, who designed the detail, wrote, "This...obtained me more applause from Members of Congress than all the Works of Magnitude, of difficulty & of splendor that surround them."

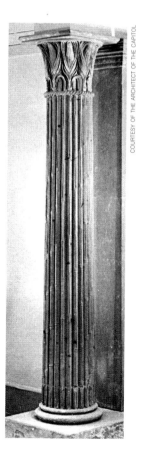

had to bear the roof load, only a fraction of the weight of a floor.

When Lenthal started work on the project, he wrote to Latrobe that he thought Latrobe's original design with nine vaults, or ribs, in the Supreme Court's ceiling would be too expensive and time-consuming to build. Lenthal suggested an alternative plan that

Old Supreme Court Chamber, lying one floor beneath the Senate Chamber, had too low a ceiling for proper arches. An early version of its dome collapsed, killing Latrobe's assistant.

eliminated the vaults and had a simple curved ceiling. Latrobe accepted the changes and seemed to absolve himself of the responsibility for the final design.

After completing the Senate-Supreme Court floor and ceiling project, Lenthal allowed the cement to dry for two months. On September 19, eager to hurry the work along, he ordered the removal of the main ceiling supports that had been left in place during the curing process. As soon as workmen began removing the supports, the ceiling began to crack and then started to collapse. All the workers except Lenthal escaped through the doors and windows before tons of brick and stone came crashing down. Lenthal was killed, and accusations and finger pointing began almost as fast as the effort to recover his body.

Latrobe admitted some responsibility for the tragedy. He acknowledged that he had agreed to Lenthal's plan, primarily due to pressure to keep down costs. It is not clear whether the design was faulty or whether Lenthal had the braces removed before the cement had fully dried. Some, like Thornton, would point to Latrobe's shortcomings as an architect and his absences from Washington as the direct cause of death of John Lenthal.

In the months leading up to the accident, the rancor between Latrobe and Thornton had become so malicious that they considered settling their differences with a duel. Thornton wanted to shoot it out, but Latrobe thought a better way of resolving their conflict would be in a court of law, even though that would leave him open to a charge of cowardice. He sued Thornton for libel for his slanderous attacks in newspapers relating to the collapsed arches and for a long list of misrepresentations about Latrobe's training and abilities. In response, Thornton hired a Maryland attorney by the name of Francis Scott Key to defend him. In 1813, after years of delay, the court vindicated Latrobe and found Thornton guilty, assessing him one penny, plus court costs.

Surprisingly, Thornton turned to writing verse while waiting for the trial, and then read some of it to the court in his failed defense. Thornton's association with his attorney may have inspired him to be a poet. Just a year later, during the War of 1812, Key would write a poem that would be put to the tune of a popular English drinking song and would become the country's national anthem.

By the time the case of *Latrobe* v. *Thornton* made it to court, the nation had been at war with Great Britain for approximately a year. Faced with pressing defense needs, Congress had deferred any additional work on the Capitol, and discharged Latrobe, who soon departed to work on other projects. When the war began, the Capitol had two well-built and richly appointed wings. Even though the acoustics were poor in the Hall of the House and the skylights leaked, the House wing proved to be a suitable space for the people's representatives. Thanks to Latrobe, the Senate and Supreme Court had equally dignified and impressive chambers. The one important section of the Capitol that remained unfinished was the Rotunda. If George Washington had lived, no doubt he would have been proud of the Capitol, but he and almost everyone else would never have guessed the fate that awaited it and the city on August 24, 1814.

A PERIOD OF FULFILLMENT TURNS TO WAR AND DESTRUCTION

Soon after work was completed on the two wings, Great Britain launched an invasion of Maryland during the summer of 1814. Two years before, the United States had gone to war with Britain during the height of the Napoleonic Wars in Europe and France's invasion of Russia. The British had become involved in a life and death struggle with the French and used "press gangs" to fill the crews of its warships, resorting to kidnapping people off the streets of Britain and forcing them to serve as sailors. They soon began stopping American ships on the high seas and taking sailors they claimed as English subjects. At the same time, while Americans were trying to settle long-standing disputes with various tribes of Native Americans in the northwest and in the south, it was believed the British were encouraging them to wage war against settlers on the frontier.

As a result, too many Americans clamored for a war that the country was ill-prepared to fight. Repeating the mistakes of the Revolutionary War, American forces attempted to capture Canada in 1812, without success. In the spring of 1813, United States Army and Naval forces launched another attack on its northern neighbor, temporarily capturing and then burning the town of York, which is modern day Toronto. When word of the burning of York reached England, some leaders wanted to exact revenge and soon found an opportunity.

By 1814, the war in Europe had ended, and Napoleon had been banished to the island of Elba. The British then turned their attention to the war in America. During mid-August, a large fleet of English warships and approximately 4,500 soldiers and marines entered the Chesapeake Bay and sailed up the Patuxent River. They landed southeast of the capital and marched under scorching sun across Maryland, where a number of the invaders died from heat and exhaustion. On August 24, the British confronted and easily defeated an American force near the town of Bladensburg, which ironically was a favorite dueling site for Washingtonians who wanted to settle disputes outside of the law.

British troops entered Washington on August 24, 1814, with little opposition, unlike this fanciful, misleading portrayal of the city.

Late that afternoon, after the bulk of American forces abandoned Washington, the British moved on the city and the Capitol. In an effort to thwart the attackers, American defenders blew up the bridges across the Anacostia River, and at approximately 8:30

COURTESY OF THE NEW YORK HISTORICAL SOCIETY

p.m., under the orders of the commanding officer, the Washington Navy Yard went up in flames with all its stores, shops, and a frigate that was under construction. About a half hour later, observers across the Potomac in Virginia and others on the heights of Georgetown reported seeing flames coming from the Capitol.

When the troops arrived at the Capitol in the early evening, a number of enlisted men and officers, surprised at the size and magnificence of the building, did not want to see it destroyed. However, Admiral Sir George Cockburn, who saw his chance to avenge the burning of York the year before, had issued the order, and after some hesitation, the soldiers started to torch the building. Their attempt failed when they tried to burn the House wing by firing what were known as Congreve rockets at the ceiling. The rockets exploded with a loud noise when they hit the ceiling but failed to ignite the roof. On a close inspection, the dismayed soldiers discovered that the chamber had sheet iron covering the roof. Undeterred, the men piled all the furniture—chairs, desks, and the Speaker's raised platform and chair— in the middle of the room and set fire to the great wooden heap, using rocket propellent. The chamber and the connecting wooden causeway soon became a raging inferno.

The same fate befell the Senate wing. Almost all of Latrobe's beautifully designed rooms and appointments, sculptures by Italian craftsmen, and a large portion of Thomas Jefferson's collection of books, the nucleus of the Library of Congress's collection, became soot and ruins. The fires in the city and at the Capitol could be seen more than 30 miles away.

The Senate wing, where the library helped fuel the fire, sustained the heaviest damage. However, some rooms escaped major damage because the soldiers had to retreat from the chambers to escape the heat and flames from other areas of the building. In several rooms, they could not finish starting fires with broken doors and window frames for fear of being trapped by the blaze. One major architectural feature of the Capitol—Latrobe's six columns and their capitals with corn motifs, located in the Senate vestibule where there was little wood to sustain a fire—survived the conflagration.

A similar fate befell the other public buildings that night and

Admiral Sir George Cockburn exhorts his troops to torch the House wing of the Capitol. "Shall this harbor of Yankee democracy be burned?" he demanded. His men piled chairs, desks, even the Speaker's platform and chair in the middle of the room, ignited them, and watched as the fire raged. The Senate wing suffered the same fate.

the next day, including the President's Mansion, executive offices, sheds, stables, and other buildings—all except one. Fortunately for the civilian population, Cockburn's orders precluded the destruction of private property. William Thornton who had become superintendent of Patents, took advantage of the exception that evening. Almost every public official had crossed the Potomac into Virginia, withdrawn to Georgetown, or moved north into Maryland to escape capture, but Thornton returned to the city once it became clear that the British intended to burn all the public buildings.* He left his wife and the safety of Georgetown and returned to the Patent Office, located about halfway between the Capitol and the President's Mansion. Standing in front of the building, Thornton confronted the arsonists and declared that the contents of the building belonged to private individuals, not to the government. Boldly, he equated the destruction of the office to the burning of the great library in Alexandria, Egypt, late in the third century, with all its collections of Greek literature, philosophy, and science. By his courage and persuasiveness, Thornton had saved the building.

Despite the efforts of the British soldiers to wreak havoc on the city that night, nature intervened to prevent total destruction of the Capitol and the President's Mansion. A timely thunderstorm helped suppress the fires. Because the two buildings were constructed of stone, which cannot withstand violent temperature changes, the weather helped avert development of serious cracks in the sandstone and marble walls and floors.

Although wet and tired, the British continued their burning the next day, but unforeseen events took a toll on the invaders. During the morning, soldiers discovered a cache of military supplies south of the Capitol and through carelessness or fatigue, accidentally set off more than a hundred barrels of gunpowder. Approximately 30 soldiers were immediately blown to bits and even more were killed or wounded by flying debris. By the afternoon, more soldiers died or suffered injury when a fierce thunderstorm or tornado struck the city. Violent winds blew down trees and chimneys, ripped off roofs, and collapsed several buildings on top of British soldiers. The ferocity of the storm weakened the morale of many soldiers who perceived the chain of events had been sent on them by divine providence.

On the night of August 25, under cover of darkness and with camp fires lit to make the residents think that they still occupied the city, the British soldiers marched back to their ships in the

*President Madison spent the night of August 26-27 approximately 20 miles north of Washington in the Quaker town of Brookville, Maryland. He stayed at the home of the man who made the silver plate for George Washington's cornerstone-laying ceremony on September 17, 1793.

Patuxent River. They sailed north on the Chesapeake Bay, planning to invade the city of Baltimore. Incensed at the destruction of Washington, angry Marylanders confronted and defeated the British forces two weeks later. When the British fleet bombarded Fort McHenry at the entrance to the city's harbor, Francis Scott Key, William Thornton's lawyer, wrote *The Star-Spangled Banner* on board a prisoner-exchange boat.

THE CAPITOL IN THE AFTERMATH OF WAr

By early fall of 1814, the inevitable question of whether to rebuild the Capitol or move to another, more secure location became a major topic of congressional debate. During the course of the contentious discussions, members met temporarily in Blodgett's Hotel, which served as William Thornton's Patent Office. Many members reminded those lobbying to move the Capitol that it was

Burned-out Capitol stands forlorn after being burned by the British. A timely rainstorm checked the flames. Some members of Congress lobbied to move the Capitol back to the more secure environs of Philadelphia.

George Washington's ardent wish to see the Capitol permanently located on its present site.

The uncertain atmosphere caused the real estate market in the city to decline precipitously. Many investors, landowners, and bankers feared that the effort to move the capital might succeed and lead to a complete collapse in land and building prices in the area. In a final attempt to thwart relocation, concerned citizens and financial interests joined in offering the government a half-million-dollar loan to be used to rebuild the Capitol.

The prospect of financial help persuaded some in Congress to reject the proposal to move. After two successful preliminary votes in the House that called for the temporary removal of the government to Philadelphia, a third and final vote failed, and the

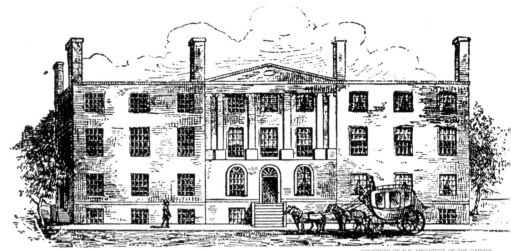

Blodgett's Hotel, a tavern across the street from the Capitol, served as a temporary home to senators and representatives while repairs were made to the heavily damaged building. Congress first convened here in December 1815 and remained until 1819, when they returned to the rebuilt Capitol.

issue came to an end. The Senate never voted on the question, but the debate in the House once again had exposed sectional differences. By a narrow margin, the southern members, along with a few Mid-Atlantic and New England representatives, kept the government from moving and prevented what certainly would have been a permanent relocation in the North. Additional sporadic attempts to move the Capitol developed several years after the Civil War and again in the 20th century, but the efforts did not gain any widespread support.

With the relocation issue finally resolved, community leaders hired Latrobe to build a temporary meeting place for the House and the Senate until permanent repairs could be made on the Capitol. The interim site selected for the new home of Congress was a tavern located across the street from the Capitol. Latrobe designed and completed work on a three-story addition to the tavern, which became known as the Brick Capitol. In December 1815, the first session of the 14th Congress convened there and paid annual rent until 1819 when work on the Capitol was far enough along for them to reoccupy the building.

Latrobe's Brick Capitol did not last, but his return to Washington heralded the beginning of finally fulfilling George Washington's vision of the Capitol. The rebuilding of the two wings and completion of the center section and Rotunda, begun under Latrobe's guidance, would be brought to fruition before the end of the 1820s. The estimated cost to repair the damage wrought by the British totaled approximately $500,000, the amount a local banker and community leaders had offered to lend to the government. In February 1815, Congress authorized the President to borrow the funds and to hire workmen to complete construction.

President Madison appointed a three-member board to man-

OLD BRICK CAPITOL

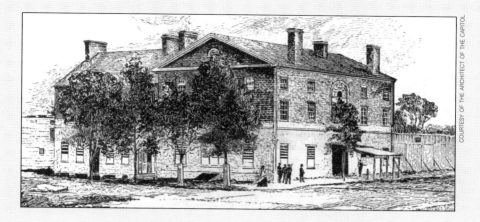

The Brick Capitol occupies a special place in American history. It was there in 1817, during the Brick Capitol's brief career as the home of Congress, that President James Monroe became the first President to hold his inauguration outdoors since Washington's first inaugural in 1789 in New York City. Just two years after the event, Congress moved back across the street into the present Capitol, and the building became known as the Old Brick Capitol. During the period between 1819 and the Civil War, the building served as a boarding house for many members while Congress was in session. One prominent senator, South Carolina's John C. Calhoun, lived in the building until he died there in 1850 at the age of 68. He served as Vice President under both Andrew Jackson and John Quincy Adams.

By the time the Civil War began, the Old Brick Capitol had fallen into disrepair, but the wartime emergency brought it back into government service when Union officials seized the building and turned it into a prison. Inmates included Southern sympathizers who could be held without habeas corpus, Confederate officers, crews from captured blockade runners, and several women spies. A few Southern women performed important wartime service for the Confederate cause by reporting information they were able to gather in wartime Washington.

As the war drew to a conclusion in 1865, the public demanded retribution for the mistreatment of Northern soldiers held in Georgia's infamous Andersonville Prison. Heinrich Wirz served as commandant of the prison, and when Union forces liberated the camp, the military charged him with several counts of murder. The Army brought Wirz to Washington where he was confined in the Old Brick Capitol. During October 1865, a military tribunal convened at the Capitol and found Wirz guilty. A sentence of death by hanging was carried out on November 10 on the lawn next to the building, within sight of the east side of the Capitol. Immediately after the execution, spectators began cutting up the scaffold and the hangman's rope. No doubt most just wanted a morbid souvenir, but perhaps some of the older generation still believed that a piece of rope from a hanging would cure headaches and other maladies. Two years later, the Old Brick Capitol was torn down, and in 1935, its site became the location of the new home of the Supreme Court.

age the rebuilding project. Charged with the responsibility to hire a professional architect, the board asked Latrobe to return to Washington to undertake the new job. Despite some initial delays on his part that did not instill confidence in the board members, Latrobe and the board finally agreed on terms, and he accepted the job. He immediately began by inspecting the condition of the Capitol and created designs for the House and Senate chambers.

Unlike his earlier experience on Capitol Hill, Latrobe did not have someone of Thomas Jefferson's stature and intellect with whom he could discuss the layout of the rooms, the artistic elements, and the structural components of the chambers. By 1815, Jefferson, no longer President, busied himself with his plantation, family, and vision of a university for Virginia. Although Latrobe was free of Jefferson's controlling influence—and his vision of how the Capitol should be completed—he now had to deal with officials of inferior imagination. Madison and, at first, Monroe proved cold and removed from the project, and Latrobe's immediate supervisors wanted to speed the work along and keep the costs from escalating.

Latrobe created the plans and executed the design for the House and Senate Chambers that are now known as Statuary Hall, or the Old Hall of the House, and for the Old Senate Chamber. He fulfilled his long-standing desire to have the House

For the new House Chamber, Latrobe fulfilled a long-standing wish and designed a semicircular room with a half-domed ceiling. It served the House for 40 years before becoming Statuary Hall in 1864—a showcase for state notables.

would be burned in the Capitol's stoves. When they went to the basement to get wood, staffers used candles or oil lamps to light the way, creating an obvious fire hazard. If the British had found such a supply of wood to use in 1814, the Capitol might have been reduced to a pile of rubble.

Bulfinch made plans to correct the danger and at the same time to address an architectural shortcoming in the Capitol's west front design. In the original plans for the west side of the building, insufficient thought had been given to how the building would look once the Rotunda section was completed. The façade projected well past the House and Senate wings, and the area that was

Its Dome in place, the Capitol begins to assume its familiar form. In 1824 it was opened to the public.

considered the basement in the wings was at ground level because of the slope of the hill. The two wings had three stories above ground, and the center section had a lower fourth level exposed, breaking the continuity of the façade. To resolve the problem, to provide a place to store firewood, and to replace the privies removed from the old wooden causeway, Bulfinch developed plans in 1826 to add a west terrace extending the width of the building and high enough to mask the ground-level windows and doors of the center of the Capitol.

After reviewing several alternative plans, Congress finally appropriated funds to build a terrace and to landscape the Capitol grounds. The plan Bulfinch completed provided a set of rooms facing the ground floor of the center section of the Capitol with a walkway on top and stairs leading down toward the mall. The design not only cut off the view from the mall of the lower floor windows, but it also allowed full use of light coming through the windows. In addition, the plan provided a convenient location for new privies, a safe, easily accessible place to store firewood, a

In October a gala reception in the Rotunda honored a visiting dignitary and old ally—the Marquis de Lafayette. Much of fashionable Washington thronged to greet him.

room for the Capitol's fire engine, and stables for the horses that pulled the engine.

One of Bulfinch's last important landscaping details was the installation of a fence around the Capitol. It was later removed, but a gatehouse used by guards and a gatepost can still be seen

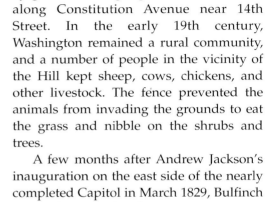

along Constitution Avenue near 14th Street. In the early 19th century, Washington remained a rural community, and a number of people in the vicinity of the Hill kept sheep, cows, chickens, and other livestock. The fence prevented the animals from invading the grounds to eat the grass and nibble on the shrubs and trees.

A few months after Andrew Jackson's inauguration on the east side of the nearly completed Capitol in March 1829, Bulfinch received notice that his services were no longer needed. Although several minor items still remained to be finished, the Capitol, as originally designed by Thornton and subsequently revised by

Colorful orator and legislator Davy Crockett works a crowd of congressmen. He served several terms in the House in the 1820s and '30s, giving many fiery— but often ineffective— speeches demanding cheap land for western settlers.

Latrobe and Bulfinch, was completed. Bulfinch had put the last touches on the Senate Chamber, where the great debates among such senators as Daniel Webster, John C. Calhoun, and Henry Clay took place. His work in the Supreme Court Chamber set the stage for the great cases of that era, including the Dred Scott decision in which the Court ruled in 1857 that a slave could not be a citizen of the United States and that Congress could not limit the expansion of slavery.

Built after the 1814 fire, the new House Chamber, like the original one, suffered from poor acoustic quality, but in spite of it, representatives were able to debate the important issues of the day. In 1823, the House learned of the Monroe Doctrine during the reading of the President's State of the Union message. Distinguished members, such as Henry Clay, Davy Crockett, and Daniel Webster, along with six future Presidents—James K. Polk, Millard Fillmore, Franklin Pierce, James Buchanan, Abraham Lincoln, and Andrew Johnson—and one former President, John Quincy Adams, worked with and against each other through the stormy sessions that confronted the divisive issues of slavery, state nullification of federal law, tariffs, and westward expansion.

"WHAT HATH GOD WROUGHT!"

Ever since Europeans began settling in America, they had continually looked west for new places to build homes and communities. As Americans moved into the sparsely populated wilderness and businessmen began establishing economic ventures throughout the country and across the Atlantic, people became frustrated by the inordinate length of time it took for a letter to travel from one part of the country to another and to and from Europe. For Americans and the British, the Battle of New Orleans tragically illustrated the drawbacks all too clearly when the final battle of the War of 1812 was fought two weeks after the peace treaty had been signed in Ghent, Belgium.

In the spring of 1844, an event at the U.S. Capitol changed all that and ushered in the modern world of almost instant communications. Sitting in a room near the old Supreme Court Chamber, Samuel F. B. Morse revolutionized communications when he tapped out the first message on his newly invented telegraph. Thus began a revolution that proved to be just as important as the creation of the spoken word and written language. Although antiquated by today's standards, the telegraph made it possible to transmit messages across vast distances by the use of electric signals sent through a wire, not unlike the Internet.

Near the Supreme Court Chamber on May 24, 1844, the telegraphic word goes forth—"What hath God wrought!"— tapped out by inventor Samuel F. B. Morse. In 1843 Morse had been granted $30,000 by Congress to build a telegraph line between the District of Columbia and Baltimore.

A multitalented individual, Morse had studied art as a young man while living in Paris and became a superb painter. During his stay in France, he studied photography under Louis Daguerre and was one of the first to open his own studio where he produced pictures using the daguerreotype process. Upon his return to America in 1833, Morse began experimenting with electricity to create a signal.

After five years, he succeeded in inventing a device that would send a message to a receiver, which recorded it on paper in a series of dots and dashes. To give meaning to the dots and dashes, he developed the Morse Code, assigning each letter and punctuation mark to a prescribed set of dots and dashes. The best known message in Morse Code is the international SOS distress signal of three dots followed by three dashes followed by three dots.

In 1843, Morse convinced Congress to appropriate the then huge sum of $30,000 to build the first telegraph line. During the following months, he hired workers to install a cable from the Capitol to the Baltimore & Ohio Railroad facilities at Mount Clare, currently a museum, in Baltimore, Maryland. On May 24, 1844, Morse clicked out his famous massage, "What hath God wrought!" to Alfred Vail in Baltimore. At the behest of a friend's daughter, Morse took the Biblical quote from the book of Numbers, chapter 23, verse 23.

During the next four years, Morse installed telegraph lines from the East Coast to the Mississippi River and from Maine to Georgia, much to the delight of most of the public. A displeased group of farmers in Kentucky, however, tore down the wires because they feared they would create an electrical disturbance and keep it from raining.

Two locomotives meet at Promontory Point, Utah Territory on May 10, 1869. The event marked the completion of the transcontinental railroad, which stitched together the two coasts and made America one.

In 1858, the first transatlantic cable was installed, but it failed within a few weeks, and a new one replaced it in 1866. During the Civil War, the country embarked on the construction of the transcontinental railroad, and workers strung telegraph lines right alongside the tracks. On May 10, 1869, the nation celebrated the joining of the eastern and western segments of the railroad at Promontory Point, Utah, when Morse's invention instantly sped the message—"Done"—to communities all across the country, signaling that the final spike had been driven, thus linking a nation that only a few years before had been torn apart by civil war.

A Growing Nation, A Larger Capitol

1850-1865

MANIFEST DESTINY AND THE CAPITOL

During Andrew Jackson's presidency, Americans began to look beyond the old frontiers. Jackson paved the way for expanding settlement in Georgia, Alabama, Mississippi, and Tennessee by forcing Native Americans to leave their ancestral homes in the south and move west of the Mississippi River.

By now, European governments had fully come to recognize the United States as a powerful and independent nation. The American people began to feel greater confidence in themselves and in their country. Settlers started streaming into the western territory, and Americans came to believe that providence had bestowed upon them a mission to settle the entire country.

During the 1840s, the concept of Manifest Destiny reached its high point, and no other President better exemplified the philosophy than James K. Polk. Many historians consider him one of the most successful Presidents, in large part because he fulfilled all his campaign pledges. He settled the Oregon boundary dispute with Great Britain, produced the first tariff bill ever drafted by the

The Capitol sits for its first known photographic portrait in 1846, a daguerreotype of the east front. The Senate wing is on the right and the House on the left. Between 1851 and 1865 the building would grow almost threefold.

executive branch, and created an independent treasury. Polk's major accomplishment was to annex Texas and to bring it into the Union, a move that led to a war with Mexico and added vast new territories to the nation, including California.

REDESIGN OF THE CAPITOL

The new territories in the west created two problems for Congress. The expansion of slavery was a major concern, and each state's delegation at the Capitol had a vested interest in the status of the new territories. Also, the admission of new states meant more members would be coming into the already overcrowded congressional chambers. The House and Senate had 57 standing committees but only 40 rooms for meetings. Members had no private offices. Typically, members' desks in the chambers were their only offices while Congress was in session. Efforts to enlarge the building before the Mexican-American War had stalled, but it became obvious that expansion of the building was inevitable. The Capitol had been completed only 20 years prior to the war, but it now needed a major enlargement to meet the needs of the growing country.

Another nagging problem for members was the poor acoustics in the House Chamber. Whenever anyone spoke in the room, the

About to sprout new wings (below), the Capitol presents a bustling scene in the early 1850s. Workmen and material clutter the site. Philadelphia-born Thomas U. Walter (above) was named Architect of the Capitol Extension in 1851.

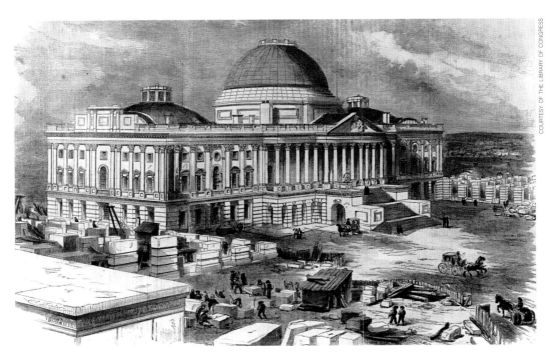

sound reverberated off the stone walls and the domed ceiling. The only way a member could be heard clearly by others was to speak standing by the Speaker's rostrum. In an effort to correct the problem, draperies were hung around the walls, the Speaker's desk was temporarily moved to the opposite end of the chamber, a visitor's gallery was added, and a temporary wooden wall was placed around the room—all to no avail. The ultimate solution was to build an entirely new wing with a chamber that had good acoustics and that was large enough to accommodate the anticipated new members.

The Senate finally set things in motion to expand the Capitol. During September 1850, as it debated and then passed the Compromise of 1850, the Senate requested its Committee on Public Buildings to recommend procedures to enlarge the building. The committee in turn asked President Millard Fillmore to take the responsibility of developing the new architectural design to present to Congress. The committee envisioned a plan that would transform the Capitol from what George Washington and Thomas Jefferson had visualized into a building nearly three times as large, constructed of the finest materials by the best craftsmen in the world.

Army engineer Montgomery Meigs, working with Walter, supervised construction of the new wings. He developed the derrick-and-crane system that installed the new Dome of the Capitol.

Numerous ideas were put forth, including one by Philadelphia architect Thomas U. Walter that called for a major addition to the east front of the Capitol that would have totally changed its appearance. The House favored the plan, but it was rejected, primarily due to the objections of Mississippi Senator Jefferson Davis. Walter presented another design on June 10,1851, that the President and both houses of Congress approved. It called for the addition of two wings of equal size on the north and south side of the building. The project would require the use of narrow corridors to connect the new wings to the original building and unify the façade. The plan met with almost immediate approval. On July 4, 1851, President Fillmore laid the cornerstone, and construction moved quickly.

Soon after President Franklin Pierce took office in 1853, he put the construction project under the control of the War Department and its secretary, Jefferson Davis. Davis supervised many of the important phases of the rebuilding plan and placed an army officer, Montgomery Meigs, in direct control of the work. Meigs, the engineer, and Walter, the architect, made important contributions to the building's redesign and its interior and exterior appointments. They moved quickly and had the House Chamber ready for members in 1857; the Senate wing was completed in 1859. However, tension had been growing between Meigs and Walter, and just months after the senators convened in their new space, the controversy came to a head. Not wishing to lose the architect and judging that Meigs was more at fault than Walter for the disagreements, John C. Floyd, Davis's successor as Secretary of War, fired Meigs on November 1, 1859.*

Congress and the nation more and more focused on the growing and nettlesome questions of sectionalism and slavery. Throughout the North and Midwest, violence had flared in a number of cities since the 1800s, especially where abolitionists were most active. Inevitably, the intense divisiveness was displayed in the Capitol.

SECTIONALISM TURNS VIOLENT

The 1850s marked one of the high points in the eloquence and enthusiasm of debate in the United States Senate. Senators Henry Clay (1777-1852), Daniel Webster (1782-1852), and John C. Calhoun (1782-1850) filled the Senate with their passionate oratory on internal improvements, nullification, expansion, and the question of slavery. Debate over slavery intensified sectional differences and inflamed the deepening division between North and South. Even the usual decorum of the United States Senate was

Savagely swinging his cane, Representative Preston Brooks of South Carolina thrashes Senator Charles Sumner of Massachusetts in the Senate Chamber. The attack came after Sumner made a vitriolic abolitionist speech, insulting Brooks' uncle, Senator Andrew P. Butler, and his state of South Carolina.

broken by a violent altercation reflecting the growing antagonism between abolitionists and Southerners.

An ardent abolitionist, Republican Senator Charles Sumner of Massachusetts delivered a scathing attack on Democratic President Franklin Pierce and three senators, including Stephen Douglas of Illinois, for crafting the concept of "popular sovereignty." The Kansas-Nebraska Act, proposed by Douglas, established a territorial government in Kansas and Nebraska and granted settlers there the right to vote on the question of slavery when they applied for statehood. Violent conflicts soon erupted in what became known as "Bleeding Kansas." John Brown and other abolitionists clashed with proslavery groups who were trying to influence the status of slavery in the Kansas territory before its admission to the Union.

Before Sumner began his speech on May 19, 1856, friends and fellow senators advised him that it was too intemperate to be delivered in the Senate Chamber and could incite violence. Standing by his convictions, Sumner blasted Pierce's policy and made a vicious personal attack on South Carolina and one of its senators, Andrew P. Butler. Sumner stated that Butler "disfigured" everything he touched and that the world would be better off if South Carolina had never existed. When Senator Douglas responded to the tirade, Sumner scoffed at his comments and said that he insulted the Senate with the "offensive odor" of his words.

After witnessing the first part of the speech and reading the text of the one delivered the next day, Preston Brooks, Butler's nephew and a member of the House of Representatives from South Carolina, decided that the rules of southern gentlemanly behavior dictated that he must thrash Sumner for his insults. Unable to find him outside the Senate Chamber on two successive days, Brooks approached Sumner at his desk once the Senate finished its business for the day and women had departed the gallery. Butler began with a verbal attack, telling Sumner that he had dishonored South Carolina and Butler's family. He then repeatedly struck the Senator on the head with his cane, leaving him dazed and bleeding.

Sumner was so incapacitated that he did not return to the Senate until three years later, during December 1859. In June 1860, he returned to his old theme and made a four-hour speech entitled "The Barbarism of Slavery." As for Brooks, only the House had authority to deal with the incident, and the vote to remove him fell short of the necessary two-thirds majority. To preserve his honor, Brooks explained the reasons for his actions and then

*During the Civil War, Meigs served as the Quartermaster General for the Union Army. His job was to supply the Army with everything it needed to operate and fight, from shoes and hats, to rifles and cannons, to paper and ink.

Early in the Civil War, troops find quarters in the Capitol. Here the Eighth Massachusetts Regiment takes over the Rotunda. The derrick used to install the Dome rises in the center of the room, and art-filled niches have been covered to protect the paintings.

resigned his seat. However, he was so popular in his native South Carolina that he proved the old maxim that "all politics is local" and was reelected to the House several months later. Partly as a result of the Sumner-Brooks affair and partly because of growing animosity among members of Congress, many representatives, senators, and guests in the galleries began carrying one or two pistols and even Bowie knives under their coats. In the name of self-defense, Congress became a virtual armory.

Union Troops Take Up Residence on Capitol Hill

In December 1860, South Carolina seceded from the Union, and other southern states soon followed its lead. Events in Washington moved quickly after April 12, 1861, when Confederate batteries around Charleston harbor fired on Fort Sumter. Three days after the fort's surrender, President Abraham Lincoln called for 75,000 volunteers, and in response to his call for troops, Virginia withdrew from the Union on April 17.

The Confederacy now extended to the banks of the Potomac River, and the Capitol had to be defended against attack. Pennsylvania volunteers arrived on April 18, and were billeted in the new House wing. The next day, the Sixth Massachusetts Regiment arrived on the Hill after battling southern sympathizers in Baltimore, Maryland, only 30 miles north of the Capitol. The regiment suffered 21 casualties—four were killed and the others were battered and bruised. The Seventh New Yorkers arrived on April 25, and the Eighth Massachusetts came the following day. The last unit to be stationed at the Capitol was the Fire Zouaves of

with decorative designs that new technology had made possible, and popular, during the Victorian period. Poole and Hunt, a Baltimore company, made a bid to produce the columns for 3.4 cents a pound. Janes, Fowler, Kirtland and Company of New York contracted to supply the remaining materials and do the installation for only 7 cents a pound. In the 19th century, no competitive bidding process existed for government contracts such as those that agencies must follow today.

The original appropriation of $100,000 granted to Walter to rebuild the Dome was recognized almost at once to be totally inadequate. By 1856, Walter began to make firmer plans and estimated that the Dome would be six inches thick and with some new masonry would weigh approximately fourteen million pounds. At seven cents a pound, the Dome would cost slightly more than one million dollars. Yet, the new Dome would only be about twenty percent heavier than the old wood and copper one it replaced.

So that the Dome would match the color of the marble and the light-colored sandstone on the façade, Walter had white paint applied to all the cast-iron pieces. The sections were painted four times prior to installation and then were touched up after final assembly. In those days, lead was used as the base for paint, and the contract called for a mixture of 25 pounds of white lead and 2 gallons of oils and driers for every 34 square yards of surface—an area of about 15 by 20 feet.

Demolition of the old Dome and construction of the new one began in 1856 with approximately 700 men working during the summer months. Construction progressed well until May 15, 1861, when the men were told to stop because the federal government could not afford to pay for both the work and crushing the Southern rebellion. Within a few days, however, Janes, Fowler, Kirtland and Company had its employees back on the job. The

Cutaway view of the Dome (opposite), designed by architect Thomas Walter, reveals a masterpiece of 19th-century engineering. Outer and inner cast-iron shells are trussed to withstand contraction and expansion. Completed, the Dome weighed nearly nine million pounds.

Columns for the new Dome reach skyward in 1857; new wings on the north and south ends near completion. Work continued sporadically throughout the war. Lincoln saw construction as "a sign we intend the Union to go on."

Oct 1857.

*Thirty-six columns—
one for each ten
degrees of a circle—
march around
the rising Dome in
the 1850s. Capitol
lore for many years
perpetuated
the mistaken notion
that the columns
represented the 36
states of the
time. To raise heavy
iron parts into place,
Meigs built a tower of
scaffolding from the
floor of the Rotunda
up through the Dome.*

COURTESY OF THE ARCHITECT OF THE CAPITOL

company had already shipped approximately 1.3 million pounds of castings that were ready to be hoisted and bolted into place, and it decided that it would have more to lose by leaving the iron lying around to be damaged or stolen than it would by putting it up without immediate and on-going payments. They took the gamble that the Union would survive and that they would eventually be paid.

That same spirit of optimism prevailed at the White House and in the halls of Congress. A year later when the government ordered all work to resume at the Capitol, President Lincoln looked upon moving forward with the construction as "a sign we intend the Union to go on."

Even as General McClellan's Army was mired in the mud east of Richmond, and with victory nowhere in sight, Congress expressed its trust in the future of the Union by passing a number of visionary bills, among them the Pacific Railroad Bill. The legislation committed the nation to build the first transcontinental railroad connecting California and the West to the eastern seaboard.

THE STATUE OF *FREEDOM*

The final, crowning element created for the Dome was the statue of *Freedom* that was placed atop the columned structure called the tholos. In 1855, Montgomery Meigs, the chief engineer under Secretary of War Jefferson Davis, asked Thomas Crawford, a prominent American artist then living in Italy, to design a work of art to complete the Dome. Crawford had already created the bronze doors for the east entrances to the House and Senate wings. He also had done the statues forming the *Progress of Civilization*, the pediment above the entrance to the Senate, and a bust of Senator Charles Sumner.

Meigs had made it clear that he did not want a statue of Washington or one symbolizing victory. Crawford then set to work creating a design he envisioned as *Freedom*, a figure victorious in war and vigilant in peace. When Meigs took Crawford's drawings to Davis, he was delighted with the proposal, except for one item—the statue had a cap that characterized a freed Roman slave. There has been conjecture that Davis rejected the image because he believed slave holders from the South would resent the symbolism, but Davis's own writings offer a different reason. While Davis's words were self-serving, they projected the Founding Fathers' concern over the danger of enslavement in the sense that people could lose their rights as freemen. He claimed that he rejected the liberty-cap concept because he and other Americans were descended from Europeans and were never slaves, and thus using the image of a freed slave would contradict history. Crawford acquiesced. The cap was replaced with a helmet crowned with an

Between design and execution, Freedom *changes hats. For the figure atop the Dome, American sculptor Thomas Crawford imagined "Freedom triumphant." Her original headdress (at left) was a liberty cap, modeled after those worn by Rome's emancipated slaves. Jefferson Davis, future president of the Confederacy, objected, and Crawford replaced the cap with a feathered headdress (right). Some still believe, erroneously, that she represents an American Indian.*

eagle's head and feathers, and stars were included around the helmet to represent *Freedom's* heavenly origin.

A full-size plaster model was completed in Rome in early 1857 from which a bronze casting would be made in the United States. The model was shipped in five pieces the following year aboard the *Emily Taylor*, an ill-maintained vessel that soon began to leak. Repairs made to the hull in Gibraltar failed to correct the problem, and the ship almost sank in the Atlantic. The *Emily Taylor* finally made it to Bermuda in July, and from there, the five parts of the statue slowly and separately made their way to Washington during the next nine months. Once in Washington, the statue was put on display in the Old Hall of the House until April 1860.

Meigs had wanted the plaster model cast in bronze on the Capitol grounds, using metal from captured British and Mexican cannons. John Floyd, then secretary of war, did not agree and ordered that the casting be done at the Clark Mills Foundry, north-

Freedom *finds her perch atop the Capitol Dome in December 1863. Her successful installation signaled the nearing completion of the Capitol expansion project, which had begun in the early 1850s.*

east of the Capitol, near the District boundary. During the course of the work, Mills had a dispute with his foreman and put Philip Reed, a first-class artisan, and also one of his slaves, in charge of the final stages of the project. By the time *Freedom* was completed and installed, Reed was freed under the District's emancipation law of 1862, and Mills received $300 in compensation. A few months after the casting was finished, the five pieces were taken to the Capitol, and on December 2, 1863, *Freedom* was fully assembled on top of the Dome. To commemorate the occasion, a 35-gun salute was fired from the 12 forts surrounding the city.

COMPLETING THE INTERIOR OF THE DOME
THE *APOTHEOSIS OF GEORGE WASHINGTON*

When Walter conceived of a Dome constructed of cast iron, he designed it with an exterior and an interior shell. The two shells would support each other through a system of intricate cross braces. As part of his design, Walter installed a ceiling in the Rotunda shaped like a large upside-down bowl and suspended from the outer shell of the Dome. He wanted visitors to the Rotunda to be able to look up and see the inside of the huge cast-iron bowl, which he envisioned covered with a magnificent work of art.

Meigs had hired an Italian painter to decorate rooms in the Senate wing in the latter 1850s, and Walter chose him to do the work on the Dome. His name was Constantino Brumidi. He had emigrated from Rome in 1852 during the political upheavals of the 1848 revolutions throughout Europe. Before coming to America, Brumidi, who was well-versed in classical art forms, had done restoration work at the Vatican. When he arrived at the Capitol in 1855, he was one of only a few artists who could paint in the delicate fresco style that Walter wanted for the Dome.

In August 1862, Walter asked Brumidi to develop a design for a painting on the ceiling of the Dome. Brumidi, he believed, was the only person in America capable of doing the monumental project in the fresco style, which required the artist to apply his paint and complete an area while plaster was still damp. To correct any mistakes or mismatching of colors, the entire section had to be removed and redone. When Brumidi completed the work in 1865, it consisted of 120 sections.

Brumidi, who had become a very proud American citizen, conceived a work of art that would glorify George Washington.

Italian painter Constantino Brumidi, hired by Meigs, arrived at the Capitol in 1855. He became an American citizen and devoted much of the rest of his life to decorating the Capitol.

Entitled *Apotheosis of George Washington*, it would show the father of the country looking down from heaven, seated between *Liberty* and *Victory*. Surrounding them, Brumidi placed 13 maidens representing the original states. On the perimeter of the shell, he

Heroic figures swirl around the Dome in the Apotheosis of George Washington, a 4,664-square-foot fresco painted by Brumidi. Forms represent the 13 original states and the Union; Washington is between Liberty *and laureled* Victory.

created six symbolic images representing *Science, Agriculture, War, Mechanics, Marine,* and *Commerce*. Each group included a central, mythical figure relating to prominent individuals, developments, and events in American history.

The location and configuration of the surface posed two problems for the artist. Since the floor of the Rotunda was 180 feet below the shell, Brumidi had to create a set of cartoons, full-size drawings of each area of the painting, that would make the figures and images seem life-size, or in some cases even larger, to the viewers below. He determined that most of the individuals in the fresco would have to be approximately 15 feet tall. Brumidi's second problem was having to deal with working on a curved surface. Since the Rotunda is 300 feet in circumference, he had to develop the cartoons so that the groupings of figures would not appear distorted or appear to run together no matter where the viewer stood in the room. Brumidi also had to calculate where to cut or fold the cartoons to assure that the flat medium would conform to the curved surface.

Brumidi was prevented from commencing his fresco because a turn of events in the Civil War delayed completion of the Dome. The exterior of the Dome was finished by December 1863, but many jobs remained undone, including stopping leaks and installing the shell Brumidi was to use for the painting. The war made it difficult to find craftsmen, and work progressed slowly until the summer of 1864. While General Lee was battling Grant's Army of the Potomac just outside Richmond, a force of Confederates under the command of Gen. Jubal Early arrived on the outskirts of Washington in early July. Early had led his troops across Maryland and had advanced to Fort Stevens on the northern edge of the city. As a result of the raid, several iron foundries in Maryland closed, and many of the unemployed men came to the Capitol to find work. With this infusion of laborers, Walter was finally able to complete the Capitol on December 5, 1864.

As soon as the Dome was finished, a construction crew built a scaffold across the top of the interior shell early in 1865. Brumidi began painting at once and completed the project in an 11-month period. He wanted to honor two people in the fresco who were most responsi-

Bearded construction supervisor Meigs appears between two businessmen in the Commerce *section of the Dome's fresco. But Meigs objected to being depicted, and Brumidi removed him.*

ble for the expansion of the Capitol and the new Dome—Walter and Meigs. He included Walter's portrait in the segment on *Science,* seated between Benjamin Franklin and Samuel Morse. He placed Meigs in the *Commerce* setting, next to *Mercury,* but Meigs thought he appeared to be accepting a bag of money from *Mercury* and requested that his image be removed.

Once Brumidi finished the painting in late 1865, he wanted to allow time for the plaster to dry thoroughly and to work on the transitions between the 120 different sections in the fresco. However, this was not to be. Edward Clark became the new Architect of the Capitol in August 1865 after Walter resigned.

Clark wanted to bring the work to an end, and despite Brumidi's pleas, the scaffold was removed. As Brumidi had feared, the transitions between the sections were visible, but the imperfections did not diminish the beauty of the composition. Although the completion of the *Apotheosis of George Washington* was viewed as the last phase of the enlargement project begun in 1850, Brumidi would spend a good deal of the remaining 15 years of his life painting in the Capitol.

ALL COURTESY OF THE ARCHITECT OF THE CAPITOL

Bronze railing features cherubs and eagles, vines and serpents. The staircase appears in both the Senate and House wings. French artisan Edmond Baudin modeled them in 1859 from designs by Brumidi.

Washington appears in classical attire in this sculpture created in the 1830s by Horatio Greenough. It was placed on the Capitol grounds but critics ridiculed it and it was removed in 1908.

The Capitol Moves with the Times

1865 to the Present

A TREASURE OF NATIONAL ART

During its history, the U.S. Capitol has become one of the most important repositories of the nation's state, or public, art. Unlike the works of many great artists that are displayed in various museums throughout the world, state art serves the function of depicting events and people to promote feelings of nationalism and are commissioned by government officials or agencies. Brumidi's *Apotheosis of George Washington* was the largest piece of state art that he completed in the Rotunda but not the last one that he envisioned.

In 1859, Thomas Walter's design of the Dome for the Rotunda included a painting around the entire 300-foot circumference of the room. Brumidi expressed a desire to create scenes recounting a series of major events in American history since 1492 in a frieze just below the large windows around the Dome. He wanted to tell the story of American history as recorded by such well-known historians as Francis Parkman, author of *The Oregon Trail*, and George Bancroft in his 10-volume history of the United States. Another important historian Brumidi would have known was William Prescott, whose works about the Spanish conquest of Mexico and Peru were popular at the time and reflected attitudes of 19th-century America.

Brumidi finally received permission in 1877 to paint the frieze.

Christopher Columbus steps ashore in the New World in a frieze by Brumidi that circles the Rotunda below the Dome. He began the massive work, which stretches for 300 feet around the room, in 1877 and completed seven panels before dying in 1880.

Within months, he had created a series of full-size sketches that began with an allegorical work entitled *America and History,* followed by Christopher Columbus's arrival in the New World. The final image of the frieze would portray the California gold rush.

Brumidi painted while standing on a small scaffold suspended from the wall, approximately 60 feet above the floor. Before he could begin work, the elderly and frail 72-year-old artist had to walk up numerous sets of stairs to get to the window level of the Rotunda and then climb down a 20-foot ladder to the scaffold. At the end of a long day's work, he had to follow the course in reverse. If he needed to leave the scaffold during the day, he had to repeat the whole laborious process. He also had to contend with the discomfort of Washington summer heat and the cold and dampness common between late fall and early spring.

After nearly two years, Brumidi had completed seven panels of the frieze and had begun working on the eighth when he had a horrifying accident. While he was painting the scene depicting William Penn signing a treaty with the Indians in 1682, Brumidi's chair suddenly tipped over. He managed to grab a rung of his ladder, preventing his fall to the Rotunda floor, and he hung there for almost 15 minutes before someone was able to pull him back to safety. He returned to the scaffold to work but never finished the Penn panel. Brumidi spent the last several months of his life doing his cartoons, and before he died in February 1880, he recommended another Italian artist to complete his painting.

Facelike image on a tree trunk, just above the fern, may be Filippo Costaggini, hired to finish the Brumidi panels. A self-portrait here might have been Costaggini's attempt to achieve immortality.

On Brumidi's advice, Filippo Costaggini received the approval of the Capitol architect to complete the panels Brumidi had planned for the frieze. By September 1880, Costaggini began work on a part-time basis and in 1889 completed the last panel Brumidi had envisioned. When he signed his name on the rock shown in the Gold Rush scene and dated it, marking the end of the project, a 31-foot gap remained between the panel and the first one Brumidi had painted. This came about because Brumidi had been told the frieze was 9-feet high; it was actually only 8-feet high, requiring a proportional shortening of the images to keep them from looking elongated. Costaggini, who had predicted the shortfall, felt that his contributions to the project were not fully appreciated because of it. His perception, whether justified or not, was reinforced when no descision was made on a set of subjects he proposed to fill the 31-foot gap.

94

A popular story about the frieze and Costaggini's perceived lack of recognition for his work centers on the tree separating the panel depicting the death of the Indian chief Tecumseh in 1813

and one showing the *American Army Entering the City of Mexico* in 1847. An image resembling a man's face appears near the base of the tree trunk between Tecumseh and the soldiers in Mexico City. Whether the image is a self-portrait by Costaggini or just a circumstance, Costaggini has achieved world-wide fame because it has become a major point of interest to thousands of Rotunda visitors.

The last 31 feet of space in the frieze remained blank for more than 50 years. In the first decades of the 20th century, Congress and the Architect of the Capitol considered several artists and a number of conflicting proposals. Finally, in 1951, Congress authorized a well-known muralist, Allyn Cox, to complete the frieze.

High above the Rotunda floor, a scaffold hangs from a railing. This one, in use around 1920, closely resembles the one used by Brumidi while painting his allegorical panels.

Conservators work at restoring the sculptured sharpness of a wall-flat fresco on the Rotunda frieze. Elaborate scaffolding supports them at their work site. Years of neglect allowed many Capitol artworks to deteriorate. Varnishes applied to many of the paintings discolored as the years went by and had to be painstakingly removed.

During the next two years, Cox created three new panels. In the first one, which focused on the Civil War, Cox painted Union and Confederate soldiers shaking hands in reconciliation instead of Generals Lee and Grant, who would have been the likely subjects in the 19th century. The second panel celebrated the Navy's contribution to victory in the Spanish American War. To complete the frieze, Cox produced a scene dedicated to flight, beginning with images of Leonardo da Vinci and ending with Orville and Wilbur Wright at Kitty Hawk, North Carolina. Once Cox completed the frieze, he began a restoration project on the other panels in an effort to return them to their original condition. He completed the work in 1954.

Over the years, paintings in the Capitol slowly deteriorated, and their restoration became an important part of the duties performed by the staff of the Architect of the Capitol. Long ago, in an effort to protect the *Apotheosis* and paintings in the Senate wing, varnishes were applied to the works in the belief that a clear film barrier would help maintain their quality. However, the varnish discolored over time, and the art gradually darkened, taking on a

yellow to light brown appearance. To repair chipped or scarred paintings, artists would touch up the damaged areas by over-painting the surface. The original work began to take on subtle changes, and with each attempt to restore a painting, it became darker and darker. As a result, Brumidi's masterpieces lost much of their original beauty over the course of a hundred years.

By the 1980s, more scientific methods of conservation and restoration had evolved. Experts in the art restoration field had developed ways to clean a painting and rediscover the original layers of paint. Specialists began the laborious process of removing all the added layers of dirt, varnish, and paint. What had become thought of as rather inferior artwork before refurbishment was once again returned to its original condition, revealing bright and diverse colors.

The restoration of Brumidi's *Apotheosis of George Washington* presented the conservators with its own set of challenges. The fresco was 150 to 180 feet above the floor of the Rotunda, and preliminary inspections showed that it would not be possible to get close enough to the painting without building a scaffold. In the mid-1980s, the architect and the House and Senate leadership authorized the construction of an elaborate scaffolding system to enable the conservators to begin a year-long project of not only cleaning the work but also improving the blending of each of the 120 sections.

They had an advantage that Brumidi probably never dreamed of: an elevator to take them from the floor of the Rotunda up to the canopy. Workers could also walk up the stairs located between the interior and exterior shells of the Dome. The stairs lead to the top of the inner Dome just below the *Apotheosis* and then up to a walkway at the top of the outer Dome at the base of the statue of *Freedom*. This was the way Brumidi had gone up to work more than a century before.

In addition to restoring Brumidi's paintings, conservators had to protect the famous work of art on top of the Dome—the statue of *Freedom*. From the time of its installation in December 1863, the bronze statue had withstood blistering summer sun and occasional subzero winter nights. As time passed, the metal oxidized and took on a greenish patina.

Freedom *goes for a ride: On May 9, 1993, after nearly 130 years atop the Capitol, the heavy statue is airlifted from the Dome and lowered to a parking lot for cleaning and restoration.*

Nautical images and motifs by Brumidi decorate the chamber that once
served as the Senate Committee Room on Naval Affairs; it has since been
turned over to the Senate Appropriations Committee. Several artists
worked under Brumidi's direction, mixing paints and painting backgrounds and ornamental designs.

In 1993, as part of the bicentennial celebration at the Capitol commemorating Washington's laying the cornerstone, a specially modified helicopter lifted all seven and a half tons of the statue from the top of the Dome and placed it on the east parking lot. Conservators immediately began a five-month-long renovation process, removing more than a century of chemical and corrosive residue. After the cleaning, workers repaired all the damaged bronze and applied a protective coat of wax. When the work was completed in October 1993, the helicopter returned, and within approximately 15 minutes of liftoff, had the statue back on top of the Dome. Since the protective wax coating only lasts a few years, conservators periodically have to climb up to the statue and apply another coat.

The statues inside the building need to be protected from a problem stemming from an entirely different source—the many visitors to the Capitol. In 1864, Congress designated the Old House Chamber as National Statuary Hall. Under the original legislation, each state was allowed to give two statues of prominent individuals to be displayed in the hall or in other areas of the Capitol. The Architect of the Capitol, who oversees the collection, has to maintain a balance between public access to the building, which ran as high as 12,000 to 14,000 visitors on peak days prior to September 11, 2001, and the conservation of the statuary collection and other art objects. In recent years, the architect's staff has stressed to the visiting public its responsibility not to touch or damage the statues. As a result of being touched or rubbed by visitors in the past, many marble statues appear to have dirty shoes, and those made of bronze have bright, shiny areas on the toes of their shoes.

Abraham Lincoln watches over Capitol business in a statue by Vinnie Ream, the first woman to receive a federal commission to produce a piece of art for the government.

A number of the statues have been under the care of the Office of the Architect for more than a hundred years, and the legislation that created the collection required that once a statue had been donated, it became the permanent property of the Capitol. In 2001, however, the law was changed to allow states to replace one or both of their statues in the collection. Many states in the late 19th and early 20th centuries selected important political or social leaders associated with their states' early history and are often unknown to today's public.

A state can now change a statue, but it must bear all the expenses of removing the old one, creating a new one, and having it moved into the Capitol. Almost as soon as the law was passed, Kansas became the first state to make a substitution. The state decided to replace the statue of George Glick, primarily noteworthy because he was Kansas' first Democratic governor, with one of a well-known favorite son, general, and President—Dwight David Eisenhower.

EXPANDING DUTIES REQUIRE NEW FACILITIES

During the later part of the 19th century and the early 20th century, society placed increasing demands on Congress. Businesses and corporations, for example, wanted to extend their influence and receive some degree of protection from regulations while a growing number of public organizations sought to limit the excess of power and money. Members found that they could no longer conduct their districts' affairs from their desks in the chambers, and working from a rooming house had never been practical. The lack of offices and the expanding number of committee meetings created a major space problem.

The first effort to alleviate the space issues came as an outgrowth of landscaping the west front terrace. After the completion of the extension and Dome of the Capitol in 1865. Thomas U. Walter retired and Edward Clark became the Architect of the Capitol. When Clark engaged the designer of New York City's Central Park, Fredrick Law Olmsted, he gave him the job of removing Bulfinch's original rooms for the fire engine, stables, firewood, and privies and replacing them with a set of conference rooms. The new areas provided members with additional space for committee hearings and meetings. As part of Olmsted's contract, he also developed a landscaping plan encompassing the entire Capitol.

Not only did members desire more space, but the Library of Congress also had more books than space on its shelves. When the library that Bulfinch designed in the 1820s suffered an almost catastrophic fire in 1851, Walter had redone the room in fire-proof cast iron. However, he could not enlarge the space to accommodate the library's growing collection. By the late 1800s, significant portions of the library's holdings were stacked in the basement without proper cataloguing or storage facilities. In 1886, Congress authorized the construction of a separate building across from the east front of the Capitol. After 11 years of construction costing more than six million dollars, Congress had a beautiful new library, currently known as the Thomas Jefferson Building. The continual growth of the collection ultimately overwhelmed the first building, and a second one was constructed in 1938. It was later named for John Adams. In 1980, the James Madison Memorial Building opened, making it the third congressional library structure on Capitol Hill.

Expanding the Library of Congress was not the only concern

of the Architect of the Capitol between 1865 and 1902. To ease the movement of members from floor to floor, Clark ordered the installation of an elevator in the building in 1874. Dozens more were added during the next 100 years. To improve the lighting inside the Capitol during the 1880s, Clark supervised the conversion from gas lamps to Thomas Edison's electric lights. Earlier experiments with electric lights on the terraces had proved unpopular because they attracted moths at night.

Clark also oversaw the modernization of the Capitol's plumbing and heating systems. In the earlier years, privies were constructed near the building, but by the post-Civil War period, toilets began to appear in the Senate wing, and bath tubs were installed in some of the basement rooms in the Capitol. Members of the House, who were considered closer to the general public, had tin tubs in their wing of the building, and senators, who were often portrayed as more aristocratic members of Congress, had marble tubs.

The Capitol was not well heated in the late 19th century, and

President Ulysses S. Grant takes the oath of office once again during his second Inaugural. The 1873 ceremony took place on the east front of the Capitol.

Early tourists visit the Capitol in a 40-passenger, 1910 electric touring bus. This image appeared in an advertisement, which touted a trip with no smoke, smells, or noise.

for Vice President Henry Wilson, one of the men who started the Memorial Day observance and who wrote the first major history of the coming of the Civil War, the combination of a bath and poor heating may have cost him his life. On a chilly, late November day in 1875, he took a bath in the basement and caught a cold. Even though the heating system in the Capitol had been upgraded from wood-burning stoves to steam heat, it still was far from adequate. Wilson later died of a "congestive chill" in the Vice President's Office near the Senate Chamber.

By the conclusion of the Civil War, few Washingtonians still owned farm animals, and parts of the fence Bulfinch had installed to keep livestock off the Capitol grounds began to disappear. The public began to picnic on the grounds, and children who lived near the Hill liked to play on the lawn. At Eastertime, they came to the Capitol grounds to hold impromptu Easter egg rolls. Frequently, they would leave egg shells in and around the Capitol, much to the disdain of the members, and in 1876, a majority of them set about to eliminate the nuisance. After two years, the House and Senate approved legislation banning picnics and egg rolling on the grounds of the Capitol. Fortunately for the children, President and Mrs. Rutherford B. Hayes invited them over to the President's Mansion for their Easter egg roll, inaugurating one of the city's oldest traditions. Now a major event, an egg roll is held every Easter Monday on the south lawn of the White House.

By the end of the 19th century, Congress once again had to address the problem of providing more office space. For more than a hundred years, members of Congress had been limited to whatever office space was available in the Capitol itself. When Elliott Woods became Architect of the Capitol in 1902, after the death of Clark, he began making plans to construct an office building for the representatives and another for the senators. Between the 1850s, when the Capitol was enlarged, and 1900, the number of representatives had risen from 243 to 391. The Senate had 28 new members, and Oklahoma, New Mexico, and Arizona were soon to be admitted to the Union.

In 1904, construction began on the House Office Building while Joseph G. Cannon of Illinois served as Speaker of the House. Considered by many historians to have been one of the most powerful Speakers in the history of the House, Cannon was the driving force behind the construction of the building. When it opened in December 1908, each member was assigned a private office. Less than three years later, in an effort to avoid overcrowding in the House Chamber and in the office building, the House of Representatives passed a legislation in 1911 to limit membership in the House to 435.

Eventually, House members needed additional space to

Peace and quiet reign in a grotto on the northwest side of the Capitol, created as a retreat from the hectic world inside. Frederick Law Olmsted, renowned landscape architect, designed it, along with the entire Capitol grounds.

accommodate ever-increasing staff needs and those of their constituents. By the 1930s, the House completed another office building that allowed members to have two-room suites. It became known simply as the New House Office Building, and its 1903 counterpart was then called the Old House Office Building. In 1955, Speaker Sam Rayburn, a Texan, wanted a third building designed, and by the end of the decade, he agreed to one that was larger than the Capitol itself. After years of controversy over its size, cost, and style, the newest congressional office building opened in 1965. The additional space provided three-room suites for each member.

In 1904, the Senate authorized the construction of its own office building approximately the same size and style of the first one built by the House. It opened in 1909, but workers did not finish its last addition and complete its façades until the 1930s.

In 1912, three years after the senators set up their offices and began conducting committee hearings as part of the legislative process, members organized an investigation, held in the third-floor caucus room, of one of the most tragic and well-known events in the 20th century—the sinking of the RMS *Titanic*. The ship was owned by the White Star Line, of which J. P. Morgan, a prominent American financier, was a principal owner.

With office space scarce, Speaker of the House Joseph Cannon promoted efforts to build a congressional office building. The first one constructed was named for him. William T. Smedley painted him in 1912.

Craftsmen in the Capitol furniture shop, photographed around 1900, build and repair chairs and desks for the members. The Capitol today offers many services, including barber shops, restaurants, television studios, and security.

11536

orizes a
ns prob-
ote how
of a site
stead of
inal ap-

MOVING TO THE NEW OFFICES.

By the mid-20th century, an expanding population brought increased demands on senators and their staffs, and they, as the members of the House had done, sought additional office space. Soon after the conclusion of World War II, the Senate began planning a new office complex that would be located across from the original Senate building, but work had to be postponed because of the Korean conflict. Construction of the new building began in 1953 when an armistice was signed and was completed five years later. By 1972, the number of Senate staffers had tripled since the end of World War II, and because of the need for even more space,

"Moving to the New Offices," a cartoon that appeared in January 1908, pokes fun at members moving their papers— including "Hopes I Still Cling To" and "Unkept Pledges to Constituents."

designers planned a third building with space for half the number of senators.

With so many office buildings and the confusion that resulted from the simple designations of "old" and "new," Congress decided to name the buildings after prominent members. Even though contemporaries of Speaker Joseph Cannon often resented his overpowering control of the House and sometimes referred to him as "foul-mouthed Joe" and a "hayseed member from Illinois," members decided that the original building should bear his name because of his leadership in its construction. The second office building, completed in the 1930s, was named for Nicholas Longworth, who also served as a prominent Speaker. The third one was named the Rayburn House Office Building for its well-known promoter. Sam Rayburn held the office of Speaker almost continuously from 1940 until his death in 1961. He helped pass the New Deal in the 1930s, and members viewed him as a great conciliatory leader. In his leadership position, he continued a tradition begun by Longworth. He would over-awe new and inexperienced members with the friendship of the Speaker while plying them with bourbon or scotch in an effort to find out everything they knew.

The Senate also began identifying its buildings. The first was named for Richard Russell, a powerful Georgia senator, who had served on the Armed Forces and Appropriations Committees. Russell would probably best be remembered for his opposition to President Lyndon Johnson's Civil Rights Act of 1964, but while

Senators and staff (below) ride an electric car built by Studebaker in a photograph taken around 1914. A tunnel connected the House Office Building to the Capitol, allowing the members to avoid bad weather.

Capitol Hill gets crowded (opposite): By 1931 the Capitol was flanked on its left by the partly finished Senate Office Building and on its right by the original House Office Building. Between it and the Capitol is the New Library of Congress and to its left is the construction site of the Supreme Court building.

Johnson was a senator in 1954, they joined forces to oppose President Eisenhower's move to help the French military in its fight against the communists in French Indo-China, now known as Vietnam, Cambodia, and Laos. Ironically, in 1965, Johnson introduced the first ground troops into Vietnam and Americanized the war in Southeast Asia.

By the 1940s an electric rail car, capable of carrying more passengers, has replaced the Studebaker.

The building completed in the 1950s was named in honor of Republican Senator Everett Dirksen, who loved to debate and used his mellifluous voice to great effect. He gained national recognition when he supported the agenda of President John F. Kennedy. Kennedy rewarded Dirksen by not helping his Democratic challenger in the 1962 Illinois senatorial race, demonstrating a maxim of representative government: Political support and loyalty sometimes trump party affiliation. The third building was named for Michigan Senator Philip A. Hart, who had been wounded on Utah beach during the D-Day landings in France in World War II. Senator Hart championed the cause of no taxation without the direct consent of the people and became known as the conscience of the Senate.

PRESERVATION V. MODERNIZATION

The Capitol has been a work in progress since its beginning in 1793. As the country grew, so did the buildings, as people and events placed more and more demands upon the legislative branch of government. By the end of World War II, a number of members of Congress had begun to press for authorization to expand the size of the Capitol to create additional offices and committee rooms. After the construction of the first congressional office building, members continually requested more facilities, but a preservationist movement began to find its voice and opposed any major changes to the Capitol.

In the 1950s, Speaker Sam Rayburn, Architect of the Capitol J. George Stewart, and others began to push for plans to expand the building. One proposal called for the addition of new and much larger House and Senate wings. Others would have created an underground parking garage and bomb shelter and a large extension of the west front, which would have required redoing the Frederick Law Olmsted terraces and landscaping.

The plan that finally passed and received funding met with almost universal approval. It harked back to Walter's 1863 proposed extension of the central portion of the east front. Ever since the change in the size and style of the Dome, from the one built by Bulfinch to Walter's cast-iron structure, it had looked off-center and appeared to be structurally unsupported. It seemed to be hanging over the center doors to the Rotunda. Although historic precedent existed sustaining the addition based on Walter's original proposals, architects and historical preservationists argued that the addition would diminish the nation's architectural legacy.

As a result of publicity about the addition and the huge cost estimates for some of the plans, the Capitol leadership finally decided to build a modest 32-foot extension to the east front, precisely replicating the original façade. Work began in 1958, and the completion of the project coincided with President Kennedy's inauguration in January 1961. One of the important stated goals, besides adding additional space, was to remove all deteriorating sandstone and replace it with much more durable marble. Since the completion of the Capitol in the 1820s, portions of the sandstone along the cornice had fallen off, and the capitals of the exterior columns were beginning to show signs of age and the effects of weather that could no longer be disguised with white paint.

Since the stonemasons from the 1790s through the 1820s had used sandstone from the same quarry on the east and west sides

"EXACTLY! WE NEED MORE SPACE"

Political cartoonist Herblock takes aim at congressional efforts to increase the size and grandeur of facilities at the Capitol. The cartoon appeared on May 26, 1977. Office buildings for both representatives and senators have now been built on Capitol Hill.

of the Capitol, the west front was also badly deteriorated. Members and architects pressed the case for more space and a redesign of the west façade, invoking the same arguments that had resulted in the east front extension. However, by the 1960s,

Model of the Capitol from the 1950s shows a projected extension of the west front. Opponents cited not only the cost, but also the fact that the old Senate wing would be buried, and no part of the original structure would be visible.

opposition to such proposals had grown in strength, due in part to the controversy over cost overruns of the Rayburn House Office Building and concern that the plan to change the Capitol's west façade exceeded anything envisioned by Walter or Olmsted. Deterioration in the stonework was obvious even to the causal visitor, but opponents wanted to find a preservationist approach to the problem instead of rebuilding the only original exterior section of the building. Their position gained support when President Johnson signed the National Historic Preservation Act in 1966. Even though Congress typically exempts itself from many of the laws it passes, members and the architect's staff could not ignore the act.

The debate continued for almost 30 years, and battle lines developed between the House leadership, which kept pressing for the extension, and the historic preservationists, several prominent architectural firms, and a majority in the Senate, including Senator William Proxmire of Wisconsin. A 1971 article appearing in the Washington *Evening Star* reported an architectural firm's estimate that the west front could be restored for no more than 15 million

COURTESY OF THE LIBRARY OF CONGRESS

Not Always Through Debate

The nation has always prided itself in the right of free speech, a free press, and a government that has consistently settled controversy through open debate and persuasion. Although the Civil War remains the one major exception in the country's history in which discussion and compromise failed, Americans on both sides of the conflict ultimately reconciled themselves to the outcome of the war and returned to the process of dialogue to settle disagreements. The precepts of debate and compromise are at the core of the nation's representative government and its method of passing laws.

In the early years of the republic, however, some Washingtonians who were unable or unwilling to settle their differences by compromise went to places like Bladensburg, Maryland, to unlawfully shoot it out with dueling pistols. Dueling became less and less frequent by the middle of the 19th century, but individual acts of violence have continued throughout the past 200 plus years, and the Capitol has been the scene of a considerable number of them.

After the British attack on Washington in August 1814, the first act of violence at the Capitol with political and governmental implications occurred when Richard Lawrence attempted to assassinate President Andrew Jackson. Amid widespread controversy, Jackson had strongly opposed a move supported by John C.

The Old Ball Game provides fun for members, who square off every year—Democrats versus Republicans. The annual baseball game still takes place today. This team from the late 1960s includes two future Presidents—Gerald Ford (far right) and George H. Bush (top row, third from the right).

"Number please." Mrs. Harriet G. Daley (opposite) became the first switchboard operator on Capitol Hill in 1908. She answered every call, and connected the caller with the correct office.

Calhoun of South Carolina that would allow a state to nullify a federal law which it considered unconstitutional. Jackson had also antagonized many powerful senators and wealthy business leaders when he dismantled the Bank of the United States, charging

President Andrew Jackson, holding a cane, confronts a potential assassin: Disgruntled constituent Richard Lawrence attacked Jackson in the Rotunda, but both of the pistols he carried misfired.

the Bank with undue economic privileges. In January 1835, Jackson went to the House Chamber to attend a funeral for a member of Congress. After the service, when the President entered the Rotunda, Lawrence moved forward and aimed a pistol at him at close range. The gun did not discharge, and Lawrence quickly pulled out a second one, but it, too, misfired. This was not Jackson's first brush with death. He carried a ball near his heart from a duel on May 30, 1806, with Charles Dickinson, who had insulted Jackson and his wife, Rachel. Dickinson paid for the insult with his life.

The Secret Service, which is responsible today for protecting the President, did not exist, and the Capitol had virtually no police or security force at the time, so Jackson and those around him had to restrain Lawrence. Because assassinating a President did not become a federal offense until after John F. Kennedy was killed in 1963, the local police and courts handled Lawrence's case. He was declared insane and sent to an asylum.

In 1850, a pistol was drawn at the Capitol a second time during an angry confrontation in the Senate Chamber. During the intense debate over the Compromise of 1850, Henry Stuart Foote in his piercing voice accused Thomas Hart Benton of treason for not supporting his fellow Southerners on the issue of slavery. At the same time, he personally insulted Benton, scorning the "nasality" in his voice. Finally, on April 17, Benton had had enough and angrily approached Foote, who beat a hasty retreat to the presumed protection of the Vice-President's chair. He drew a pistol and started waving it in the air, further incensing Benton, who dared Foote to fire. Several members quickly restrained the two antagonists while others ducked for cover.

The two senators had displayed conduct unacceptable in the chamber, and as a result, a committee determined that the Senate needed to impose rules on members and restrict verbal abuse. Keeping in mind the frayed relationship that existed between the proslavery and antislavery factions, the Senate decided not to censure either senator and urged greater civility among members. However, the committee's recommendations did not entirely stop the name calling and slanderous speech, which led to one of the most notorious incidents in the Senate's history: Preston Brooks' attack on Charles Sumner in 1856. (See pp. 78-80.)

After the rancor of the 1850s and the threat of invasion during the Civil War, the Capitol remained relatively quiet until February 1890, when the first murder took place. It came as a result of a sex scandal involving a former member of Congress and a newspaper reporter. Members of the press and of the government have long argued about what is private and should not be publicized and what is public and should be open to scrutiny. In this instance, an article revealing a former member's personal conduct resulted in murder. It took place on the steps in the House wing leading from the main floor, where the House Chamber is located, to the ground level and the carriage entrance on the east side of the Capitol.

Representative William P. Taulbee of Kentucky, a former Methodist minister who was recognized for his skill as an orator, arrived in Washington in 1885. Shortly afterward, he became involved in a torrid affair with a woman who worked in the Patent Office. The Washington *Evening Star* published an account of the congressman's activities that became known as the Patent Office Scandal, but Taulbee succeeded in suppressing the story back home for approximately a year with the help of his fellow members from Kentucky. However, in 1888, Charles Kincaid of the Louisville *Times* reprinted the story in Kentucky papers, ruining Taulbee's political career as well as ending his marriage.

Taulbee, who retired and became a lobbyist on Capitol Hill, later met Kincaid in the halls of the House wing. Taulbee, a large man, attempted to drag Kincaid outside to settle the matter with fists, even though Kincaid had offered him an opportunity to publish a rebuttal statement in the Louisville papers. Kincaid, who was a smaller person, escaped after Taulbee grabbed and threatened him. He stayed away from the Capitol and Taulbee until the beginning of the new congressional session in 1889.

*Speaker of the House
Thomas S. Foley, in
the highest seat on the
dais, presides over
the House of
Representatives in
1990. Leaders of the
majority party and the
minority party use
the tables in the third
row of the chamber.
The House has met
here since 1857.*

According to an account in the *Washington Post* on March 1, 1890, the two accidentally met on February 28 near the east entrance of the House wing. Taulbee grabbed Kincaid by the lapel, threatened him, and told him that if he did not want to fight, he had better get a gun. Some accounts suggested that he grabbed Kincaid by the ear or the nose, but the doorkeeper of the House denied those reports. Kincaid left the building and returned shortly with a revolver.

The fatal encounter took place in the House wing as Taulbee neared the bottom of the stairs and saw Kincaid. When Taulbee renewed his threats, Kincaid quickly drew his pistol and fired a single shot at him, hitting him near his left eye. Physicians immediately attended to Taulbee and had him taken to a local hospital. Initially, the wound was thought to be non-life threatening, but a doctor discovered that Taulbee could not anesthetize, precluding removal of the bullet and ensuring his ultimate death. Taulbee remained conscious throughout the entire ordeal, and died on March 11.

Authorities temporarily jailed Kincaid, but he was released on bond that was raised by his fellow correspondents. He was later acquitted, partly because of the pretrial publication of newspaper stories supporting his claim of self-defense and pointing out that Taulbee never asked the police to press charges while he lay dying in the hospital. In Capitol lore, the story persists that several spots on the marble steps where the shooting took place are stains of Taulbee's blood.

Many years later, two separate incidents occurred that involved handguns, distressed individuals, and members of Congress. In 1932, a man in the House visitor's gallery began brandishing a pistol, demanding to speak to the assembled membership. After negotiations between Representative Melvin Maas of Minnesota and the gunman, Marlin Kemmerer, the situation was resolved peacefully, and Kemmerer was taken to jail. In 1947, William Kaiser, who had worked on the Capitol police force and who had suffered a substantial loss of money when an Ohio financial institution went out of business, tried to kill Senator John Bricker from Ohio. Kaiser fired two shots at the senator near the subway connecting the Capitol and the Senate Office Building. Fortunately for the senator, both shots missed.

On March 1, 1954, another shooting took place at the Capitol, but this time several shots found their mark. One of the best-known cases of violence in the history of the building occurred when four Puerto Rican nationalists came to Washington via New York City intent on shooting up the House of Representatives and publicly proclaiming to Congress their demand for a free and independent Republic of Puerto Rico. Expecting to die in the attack, they had no return tickets. The nationalists were part of a small political group that wanted the United States to give up occupancy of Puerto Rico. Two members of the faction had failed in an attempt to assassinate President Harry Truman in 1950, leaving one attacker and a police officer dead and the other attacker in jail for life. In a move the faction opposed, the United States and members of the majority political party declared Puerto Rico a Commonwealth on July 25, 1952, the anniversary of America's occupation of the island in 1898.

In March 1954, four Puerto Ricans—three men and a woman—entered the House gallery armed with pistols during a debate that focused on immigration. According to one account, just after a member referred disparagingly to Mexicans as "wetbacks," the three men in the gallery fired approximately 30 times at representatives. They peppered the entire chamber with bullets and wounded five members before Capitol police overwhelmed them.

Capitol Police officers lower the flag over the east front to half staff, honoring two fellow officers—John Gibson and Jacob Chestnut—killed in the line of duty on July 24, 1998. A mentally ill man entered the building and immediately began firing.

The officers quickly arrested the men and their woman accomplice, who had planned the attack. The four later stood trial and eventually went to prison. They remained there until 1979 when President Jimmy Carter acceded to public opinion in Puerto Rico that contended the inmates had served sufficient time, and issued a pardon on the condition that they not engage in further violence. That September, they returned to a jubilant crowd of well-wishers who still sought independence even though the island had its own elected delegate in Congress.

One of the most tragic events ever to occur at the Capitol involved the shooting death of two Capitol police officers late on a Friday afternoon, July 24, 1998. Armed with a pistol, a man named Russell Weston, who had a history of paranoia and

*An explosion rocks
the Capitol on March
1, 1971: A bomb con-
sisting of 15 to 20
pounds of dynamite,
placed in the oldest
part of the Senate
wing, caused some
$200,000 in damage.
It wrecked an
unmarked men's room
and gutted the
Senate's four-seat
barbershop. Protesters
opposed to the U. S.
incursion into Laos
during the Vietnam
War planted
the bomb.*

schizophrenia, entered the building through a ground-level entrance then known as the Document Doors. When he went through the security check, the alarm sounded, and he immediately started shooting and running toward a door that led to the office of the House Majority Whip. In the initial exchange by the outside door, Office Jacob Chestnut, a Vietnam veteran, was mortally wounded, and a visitor was hit in the face and shoulder.

After Weston got away from the security checkpoint, he quickly turned and ran into the Whip's office where Special Agent John Gibson confronted him. Approximately 20 shots were fired and by the time the exchange ended, both men had suffered a number of wounds. Gibson later died in a hospital. Weston, who sustained injuries to his body and head, survived. Senator William Frist of Tennessee, a doctor, tended to Gibson and Weston before medics took them to a hospital.

As a lasting tribute to the two officers, Congress changed the name of the Document Doors to the Memorial Doors and accorded the officers the honor of lying in the Rotunda, a rare privilege granted in the past to such notable American's as Henry Clay, Abraham Lincoln, John F. Kennedy, and the unidentified soldiers, sailors, and airmen of the two World Wars and the Korean conflict.

The Capitol has also been the scene of three major bombings during the 20th century. Even though they caused some damage to the building, none of the bombs resulted in injuries or disrupted the work of Congress. Ironically, all three were perpetrated by individuals who opposed the use of military force in international affairs but who resorted to war-like tactics themselves in an effort to influence national policy.

During the first three years of World War I (1914-1918) the United States took a public position of neutrality until the nation declared war on Germany in April 1917. American trade policy permitted commerce with any nation, but Britain had established a naval blockade of Germany, that, in effect, favored the English. On May 7, 1915, the Germans, after issuing public warnings that they would use submarines to attack all ships carrying arms, including passenger liners, sank the RMS *Lusitania* off the Irish coast with the loss of approximately 1,200 persons, including 128 Americans.

Apparently angered by what he perceived as a pro-British atmosphere in the nation, particularly in the business community and Congress, a German-born individual named Erich Muenter planted a primitive bomb near the Senate Reception Room. It exploded at 11:23 p.m., July 2, 1915, and caused only minor damage.

By the following morning, Muenter had traveled to New York where he went to the home of American financier J. P. Morgan, who was breakfasting with the British ambassador. Using two pistols, he forced his way into the home and shot Morgan, inflicting two nonfatal wounds. During the fracas, Morgan's butler knocked Muenter unconscious with a lump of coal. After his arrest, the police took Muenter to Nassau County jail, where he committed suicide on July 6. Before his death, he confessed to planting the bomb at the Capitol.

Senators gather in the Chamber where they have assembled since 1859. Sixty-six Senators arrived then; today 100 meet. They are seated by party affiliation and by seniority: The Majority party—in this case, Republicans—are in the foreground; the Democrats sit across the aisle. In most cases, the members with most seniority sit nearest the podium.

Almost 56 years later, the Capitol again became a target during one of the most contentious periods of 20th century American history. On March 1, 1971, at approximately 1:30 a.m., a bomb exploded in the Old Senate wing and badly damaged several rooms. Although no one claimed responsibility for the crime, it was believed to be the work of antiwar activists who were opposed to the government's policy in Vietnam. The bombing occurred in the aftermath of the controversial incursion into Cambodia and the killing by National Guard troops of four Kent State University students during a protest to the war. Both actions led to increased resistance to the conflict.

On November 7, 1983, an explosive device blew up near the Senate Chamber on the second floor. America had become involved in conflicts in Lebanon and Grenada, and a group referring to itself as the "Armed Resistance Unit" had set off the bomb in objection to American international policy. The blast took out a wall, damaged two chandeliers, dislodged the door to Senator Robert Byrd's office, shattered the windows in the Republican cloakroom, and broke the "Ohio Clock," so-called for the 17th state because of the 17 stars on its face. The explosion also tore apart a painting of Daniel Webster, leaving the image of his head on the floor, but the curator saved it before it was thrown out with debris left from the explosion.

A lengthy FBI investigation in 1985 led to a Baltimore apartment full of weapons, bomb-making components, and false identification materials, and a grand jury brought charges against seven people for a string of bombings in New York City, Washington, D.C., and the Capitol. The defendants had been involved with a student group in the 1960s known as the Students for a Democratic Society, which, by the late 1960s, had splintered into the more radical Weather Underground faction that advocated the use of violence. These groups became involved in student protests at several major colleges and universities across the country against racial intolerance, militarism and the Cold War, and what they defined as imperialism. During the trial, defendants initially denied the charges, but they later pled guilty. In the proceedings, they stressed that no one had been killed or injured in the bombing at the Capitol, but the court was unmoved, and they were sentenced to lengthy jail terms. In the aftermath of the bombing, the Capitol police installed electronic screening devices at all entrances to the Capitol, congressional office buildings, and the Library of Congress.

So far, most of the bombings and shootings have been assaults on individuals representing the people of the nation or acts of protest against national policy. None has risen to the level of a major attempt to destroy the Capitol. Not until September 11,

Her war vote proved unpopular with many voters, but it did not dissuade her from running for a Senate seat two years later. Rankin lost the race, but after taking a long break from Washington, she decided to run for a House seat in 1940. She won one of the two seats from Montana and assumed her new position in January 1941. In less than a year, on Sunday afternoon, December 7, 1941, Rankin realized she would have to vote yes or no to declare war, this time against Japan.

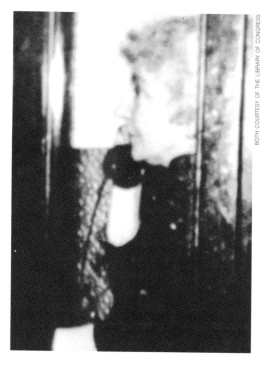

The next morning, President Franklin Roosevelt called Congress into a special session to ask for a declaration of war. Before the President arrived, Rankin had made up her mind that she would oppose the declaration and her position was already well known around Capitol Hill. Prior to the call of the roll, she tried but failed to get the Speaker's attention in an effort to explain her position to her fellow members and the public. As the roll was called, tension rose in the House Chamber, on the floor and in the galleries, in anticipation of her lone "no" vote. When she attempted to make her way back to her office, so many angry individuals besieged her that she had to seek refuge in a phone booth where she called the Capitol police to rescue her.

As a result of the unpopularity of her vote, Rankin did not run for reelection and stayed out of public affairs until the late 1960s when she reemerged and joined the anti-Vietnam War movement while in her late 80s. At the time of her death in 1973, 16 women served in the House, including the first African American, Shirley Chisholm, who was the first black member to launch a serious campaign to run for the White House in the 1972 Democratic primaries. In honor of Rankin's groundbreaking efforts for equal rights and world peace, the state of Montana placed a statue of her in the Capitol in 1985.

On November 21, 1922, Rebecca Felton, a Democrat from Georgia, became the first woman to serve as a United States Senator. She had been appointed by the governor to finish the term of a senator who died in office. At the age of 87, Felton set the record for being the oldest person to become a senator, and she also earned the distinction of having the shortest senatorial career, serving only one day.

It has been a long Senate tradition for women to come to the office through the death of a sitting member, usually a husband.

Calling for help, Representative Jeannette Rankin takes refuge from an angry crowd in a phone booth. She had just cast the only vote opposing President Roosevelt's call for a declaration of war against Japan on December 8, 1941.

Of the more than 30 women who have served as senators during the 20th century, 13 came by way of appointments by state governors after the death of a sitting member. The second woman to become a senator, Hattie Caraway of Arkansas, succeeded her husband in 1931, and she was elected to two more terms. She left office in January 1945. Known as "silent Hattie" because she made no Senate speeches, Caraway nonetheless took a strong stance on issues of concern to Arkansas, supporting prohibition and voting against anti-lynching legislation.

Magaret Chase Smith of Maine was the first woman to be elected on her own to the Senate. After completing the House term of her deceased husband, Smith served four more terms and in 1948 was elected to the Senate. She ran successfully three more times before being retired by the voters in 1972. Smith earned the title of "Mother of the Waves" for her efforts to promote the status of women in the Navy. She also played a major role in the passage of a 1948 law that provided women in the military with equal pay, rank, and privileges. Her 1950 Senate speech, "A Declaration of Conscience," strongly denouncing the inflammatory tactics of Senator Joseph McCarthy's anticommunist crusade, gained national recognition.

By the start of the 21st century, women held Senate seats from states throughout every region of the nation, and in California, Maine, and Washington State, women held both seats.

People of Spanish heritage, who by the 21st century, constituted the largest minority of the population, have a long history in America and of service in Congress.

Montana honors native-daughter Jeannette Rankin, the first woman to serve in Congress, with a likeness in Statuary Hall. Fiercely anti-war, she had voted against U. S. entry into both World Wars and, in her 80s, protested the Vietnam War.

The oldest city in the United States, St. Augustine, Florida, was established in 1564 by the Spanish, and Santa Fe, now the capital of New Mexico, was founded three years after the English built their first permanent settlement at Jamestown, Virginia, in 1607. Florida, the oldest state in the Union with a strong Spanish heritage, elected the nation's first Hispanic to Congress in 1822. After the Mexican-American War of 1848, the United States added vast new areas to the country that were populated primarily by people of Spanish and Native American descent. The territory of New Mexico became the first region in the newly acquired lands to send a Hispanic to Congress. Jose Manuel Gallegos came to Capitol Hill in 1853 and served one term as the territory's delegate. After leaving Congress, he returned to New Mexico, but Confederate troops from Texas imprisoned him in 1862 because of his support for the Union. After Gallegos' release, he held other territorial offices, and he returned to the House in 1871 to serve another term as the territory's delegate.

In 1936, the people of New Mexico elected the nation's first Hispanic to a full term in the Senate. Dennis Chávez actually began his senatorial career in 1935 through an appointment to fill a vacancy, and voters returned him to Washington in the next election for a six-year term. During his career, he worked toward extending fair employment rights to all citizens and sought fair treatment for Puerto Rico. New Mexico continued to reelect Chávez to the Senate through the 1940s and 1950s until his death during the fifth term in 1962. As a final tribute to Chávez, his statue, the first from New Mexico, was placed in National Statuary Hall.

Reflecting their growing numbers and political influence, Hispanic members of Congress formed the Congressional Hispanic Caucus in 1976. During the final two decades of the 20th century, membership in the caucus included the first Cuban-American and representatives from Arizona, California, Illinois, New Jersey, and Texas; and delegates from Guam and Puerto Rico. Hispanic members have served on a wide range of committees, including Armed Services, Intelligence, Education, Small Business, Agriculture, and the very important Appropriations Committee that decides how taxpayers' money is spent.

Although Native Americans have a long and proud history, they have had to overcome major adversities and prejudices since the 17th century to achieve political recognition.

One of the most famous Americans of the 19th century, Sam Houston, became an adopted member of the Cherokee Nation in the early 1830s. Before he moved to the Indian Territory, the people of Tennessee had elected Houston governor and had sent him to Washington for two terms as a congressman during the presidency of John Quincy Adams. In 1835, he left his adopted Cherokee people and moved to Texas where he fought for Texan independence from Mexico. Houston became the first president of the Republic of Texas, and with the state's admission to the Union, he was elected to the Senate. He served from February 1846 until March 1859, during the contentious debates leading up to the Compromise of 1850 and the Kansas-Nebraska Act of 1854. After he left Congress, Houston was again elected governor but was forced from office when he spoke out strongly against the Texas secession from the Union in 1861. Although Houston's refusal to support the Confederacy caused many

Native American scholar and leader Sequoya, a member of the Cherokee nation, was a gift to Statuary Hall from Oklahoma in 1917. Sequoya devised an alphabet that allowed the Cherokee language to be written and read.

Texans to turn against him at the time, the state paid tribute to him in 1905 by placing his statue in National Statuary Hall.

The statue of another well-known Native American has been set in a place of honor in the Capitol near the House Chamber. The state of Oklahoma honored Will Rogers who was part Cherokee and who overcame his humble beginnings as a cowboy to become a nationally renowned writer, humorist, and motion picture star. His son, William Vann Rogers, Jr., served as a member of the House, representing California from January 1943 until May 23, 1944. He spoke out frequently before and during his congressional career against Nazi atrocities and especially the Nazi treatment of European Jews. He resigned from his congressional seat to join the Army during World War II. After receiving a Bronze Star and Purple Heart during the Battle of the Bulge and facing combat in Germany, Rogers ran unsuccessfully for one of California's Senate seats, and he later served as Commissioner of Indian Affairs.

COURTESY OF THE ARCHITECT OF THE CAPITOL

Folksy philosopher and humorist Will Rogers was another gift from Oklahoma. Sculptor Jo Davidson cast him as a relaxed and easygoing figure. "I tell you folks," he once said, "all politics is applesauce."

Charles Curtis, another Native American who served in Congress, represented the state of Kansas and later rose to the second highest office in the nation. He was born into the Kansan tribal group in 1860, but his Indian grandmother persuaded him to leave the tribe shortly after his mother's death and live with his non-Indian grandmother so that he might have greater opportunities for advancement. Curtis became a lawyer in 1881, and because of his outstanding community work, the Republican Party nominated him to the House of Representatives in 1884.

Curtis won the November election, and he returned to the House for six more successive terms. During January 1907, he left the House and took a seat in the Senate. His fellow Republican senators held Curtis in such high regard that in 1911 they elected him President pro tempore of the Senate, the presiding officer in the chamber when the Vice President is absent. Even though he had risen to such a prominent and important position, he lost his bid for reelection and left the Senate in March 1913. Before adoption of the 17th Amendment to the Constitution, state legislatures and governors elected senators. After the Amendment passed, the people of Kansas could directly elect their senators, and Curtis was reelected in 1915. During his second senatorial career, he served on numerous committees, and his fellow senators elected him Senate Majority Leader.

In 1929, Curtis became Vice President of the United States, serving under President Herbert Hoover. As President of the Senate,

Curtis supported the administration and presided over a Senate in turmoil during the national crisis brought on by the Great Depression. In 1935, a bust of Curtis joined those of other Vice Presidents displayed in niches around the Senate Chamber and in the hallways of the Senate wing.

The large, imposing statue of King Kamehameha I, presented to the Capitol by the state of Hawaii, symbolizes a group of people—the Asian Pacific Americans—that has become a major force in the nation's social and political life. The group includes individuals and their descendants from eastern and Southeast Asia and from a wide range of Pacific islands, now territories or commonwealths of the United States.

As a group, the people from East Asia and the Pacific islands have endured a long history of discrimination and exclusion from the political system. It began with the first large migration of Chinese to California soon after it became a state in 1850. During the construction of the first transcontinental railroad, owners of the Central Pacific Railroad sought all the Chinese workers available in the state to build the rail line toward Utah and the junction with the Union Pacific. They even sent agents to China to encourage men to move to California to become part of the workforce. However, by 1882, their labor was no longer needed, and European Americans in California persuaded Congress to pass the Chinese Exclusion Act that ended most Chinese immigration into the country.

The exclusion policy and international aspirations of the United States to become a world power came into direct conflict during the 1890s. The Spanish American War and the expansionist policies of the period demonstrated the dichotomy of taking possession of territories with divergent populations while limiting participation in national political affairs almost exclusively to European Americans. In 1898, President William McKinley annexed Hawaii, and it became an American territory in 1900. Congressional policy granting territories the right to have a representative in the House opened the door for the first person of Asian-Pacific heritage to come to Capitol Hill.

On March 4, 1903, Jonah Kalanianaole replaced William Wilcox in the House as Hawaii's delegate, a position he held until his death in 1922. A member of the royal Hawaiian family, Kalanianaole had fought against an American-led revolution in Hawaii and had spent a year in jail before leaving his native islands to join the British Army fighting the Boers in South Africa. In 1901, he returned to the islands and decided that the best way to help his people would be to work within the political system.

Native American Charles Curtis rose from humble beginnings in Kansas to be Vice President of the U. S. under Herbert Hoover. Born a member of the Kansan Tribal Group in 1860, he was elected to the House in 1884 and served in various capacities until 1929.

U. S. SUPREME COURT
AT THE CAPITOL 1800 -1935

Before it had a building of its own, the U. S. Supreme Court met in the Capitol. Between 1810 and 1860 the justices convened here, in a room directly below the Senate Chamber.

THE COURT FROM 1800 TO 1810

When the justices of the Supreme Court arrived in the federal city in 1801, they had to share a committee room on the first floor of the unfinished Capitol with the Senate or a room used by the House of Representatives and the Library of Congress. There were only six justices on the Court from 1789 until 1807, and they had become accustomed to sharing a chamber with legislators in Philadelphia. In 1803, that Court handed down one of the most important and far-reaching decisions in American history in the *Marbury* v. *Madison* case, establishing the precedent that the Court could declare a federal law unconstitutional. Thomas Jefferson proposed and Congress agreed in 1807 to increase the number of justices to seven.

THE SUPREME COURT MOVES INTO
ITS OWN CHAMBER: 1810-1859

Beginning in 1810, the Court met in its own chamber on the first floor of the Capitol directly below the Senate Chamber, except during the years between 1814 and 1819 when the Capitol was being rebuilt after it was burned by the British in the War of 1812.

Seven justices sat on the Court until 1837, when Presidents Andrew Jackson and Martin Van Buren each appointed one new justice to the bench and increased the total to nine.

In one of the Court's seminal decisions during this period, Chief Justice John Marshall, in 1819, established the supremacy of the federal goverment over the states in *McCulloch* v. *Maryland*, and in *Gibbons* v. *Ogden* in 1824, he established the power of the federal government to regulate interstate commerce, which much later would be one of the tools used during the civil rights movement to achieve

integration. In 1857, Chief Justice Roger B. Taney handed down the *Dred Scott* v. *Sanford* decision that strongly intensified sectional differences over slavery.

THE COURT MOVES AGAIN: 1860-1935

From 1860 until the Court moved into its own building in 1935, the justices met in the Old Senate Chamber. In 1863, Congress and President Abraham Lincoln expanded the number of justices to ten, but while Andrew Johnson served as President, Congress reduced the number to eight. Then, soon after Ulysses S. Grant became President, William Strong was named the ninth judge on the Court. Not since Franklin D. Roosevelt's 1937 court-packing plan to increase the number of justices to as many as 15 has there been a serious effort to change the Court's size.

Two important cases heard during the period involved civil right's issues. In 1896, the Court handed down the *Plessy* v. *Ferguson* decision, establishing the concept of separate but equal public facilities. In the *Buck* v. *Bell* case of 1927, the justices upheld sexual sterilization laws that allowed states to sterilize the mentally incompetent, a case cited during the Nuremberg trials, justifying Nazi eugenics.

Old Senate Chamber served as the Court's home beginning in 1860. The more flamboyant decorations, as well as the visitor's gallery, were removed in order to suit the more somber nature of the Court.

BOTH COURTESY OF THE ARCHITECT OF THE CAPITOL

As a delegate in 1919, he sponsored the first legislation to make Hawaii a state, and he fought for the Hawaiian Homes Commission Act that provided for native Hawaiians to create their own homesteads. The act was designed to help insure the survival of native islanders and to protect their land from the powerful pineapple and sugarcane interests.

After the conclusion of World War II in 1945, other Asian Pacific Americans began to enter national politics. With the admission of Hawaii as the 50th state in 1959, the citizens elected Hiram Leong Fong as one of the state's two new U.S. senators. Fong holds the distinction of being the first person of Chinese ancestry to be elected to Congress. In May 1990, Daniel Akaka became the first native Hawaiian to become a U.S. senator.

Before the end of the 20th century, two other Pacific islands under American jurisdiction gained delegate representation in Congress. The Samoan Islands, located south of the equator and midway between Hawaii and Australia, became an American territory in 1904, but it was not until 1980 that Congress passed legislation granting Samoa the right to send a delegate to Washington. Samoans chose Fofó Fiti Iosefa Sunia to represent them and he took office the following year. A native Samoan, Sunia had served in a number of government positions and was involved in the island's tourism and publishing interests before serving four terms in the House.

KAMEHAMEHA

Statuary Hall's most striking figure, Hawaii's King Kamehameha I, stands tucked into a corner. Thomas R. Gould created the colorful figure, which was dedicated in 1969.

Guam, an island in the Marianas, came under American control as a result of the Spanish-American War. Under a 1972 law, the people of Guam became citizens but without the right to vote in national elections. They were, however, granted the right to send a delegate to Congress, and they elected Antonio Borja Won Pat to represent them. Like his fellow delegates from Samoa and those from Puerto Rico, the Virgin Islands, and the District of Columbia, Won Pat had all the privileges of congressional membership, including working and voting in congressional committees, but could not vote with the full House on national legislative issues.

Epilogue

The extension of equal rights and representation in Congress to all Americans, regardless of their gender or ethnic heritage, has a long history. When the Founding Fathers established the federal government and began building the U.S. Capitol in 1793, European American males were the primary beneficiaries of all the rights and privileges of citizenship. The residents in slave-holding states received the additional advantage of having their representation in the House increased by three-fifths for each African American held in slavery. As the nation has evolved during the past 200 years and the rights of citizenship have been expanded in the fulfillment of the ideals expressed in the Declaration of Independence and the Constitution, the Congress and the building where it conducts the nation's business, the U.S. Capitol, have also evolved.

The Capitol is constructed of stone and cast iron, but that only speaks to its physical nature. As the home of our elected representatives, the building, with its varied architectural styles and its extensive art collection, is a reflection of the nation, past and present. Some national leaders wanted to commemorate George Washington's contribution to the construction of the building by placing his body and that of his wife under the floor of the Crypt in the Capitol, but family members declined the offer. Washington, who adhered to the concept of progress and believed that a leader should "discharge the relative duties to his Maker and fellow men without seeking any indirect or left-handed attempts to acquire popularity," would have objected to turning the Capitol into a mausoleum and a shrine. Today, many paintings throughout the building honor the father of the nation, and the Capitol remains what Washington envisioned—a working and evolving forum where the people speak.

Directly below the Rotunda, the Capitol Crypt displays memorabilia of the Capitol's history, construction, and furnishings. An early plan would have made it the burial site of George and Martha Washington. A compass stone marks the exact center of the Capitol, the point from which Washington's streets are numbered and lettered.

Bibliography

Aikman, Lonnelle. *We, the People: The Story of the United States Capitol.* Washington, D.C.: U.S. Capitol Historical Society, 2002. 144 pp. (F204.C2A45)

Allen, William C. *The United States Capitol: A Brief Architectural History.* Washington, D.C.: Government Printing Office, 1995. 36 pp. (NA4411.A58)

_____. *History of the United States Capitol: A Chronicle of Design, Construction, and Politics.* Washington, D.C.: Government Printing Office, 2001. 461 pp. (F204.C2A458)

_____. *The Dome of the United States Capitol: An Architectural History.* Washington, D.C.: Government Printing Office, 1992. 81 pp. (NA 4411.A58)

Architect of the Capitol. *Art in the U.S. Capitol.* Washington, D.C.: Government Printing Office, 1976. 428 pp. (N6535.W3U54)

Arnebeck, Bob. *Through a Fiery Trial: Building the Capitol: 1790-1800.* Lanham, Md.: Madison Books, 1991. 628 pp. (F197.A76 1990)

Baker, Richard Allan. *The Senate of the United States: A Bicentennial History.* Malabar, Fla.: Kreiger, 1988. 255 pp. (JK1158.B35)

Bedini, Silvio A. *The Life of Benjamin Banneker: The First African-American Man of Science.* Baltimore: Maryland Historical Society, 1999. 428 pp. (QB36.B22B4 1999)

Bowling, Kenneth. *Creating a Federal City, 1774-1800.* Washington, D.C.: American Institute of Architects Press, 1988. 112 pp. (F204.C2B66)

Currie, James T. *The United States House of Representatives.* Malabar, Fla.: Kreiger, 1988. 228 pp. (JK316.C87)

Frary, I.T. *They Built the Capitol.* Richmond: Garrett and Massie, 1940. 314 pp. (F204.C2F7)

French, Francis O. *Growing Up on Capitol Hill.* Edited by John J. McDonough. Washington, D.C.: Library of Congress, 1997. 80 pp. (F202.C2F74)

Fryd, Vivien. *Art & Empire: The Politics of Ethnicity in the United States Capitol, 1815-1860.* 1992. 213 pp. (N6535.W3F78)

Green, Constance McLaughlin. *Washington.* Vol. 1: *Village and Capital, 1800-1878,* Vol. 2: *Capital City, 1879-1950.* Princeton, N.J.: Princeton University Press, 1962. 445 pp. and 558 pp. (F194.G7)

Greenberg, Ellen. *The House and Senate Explained: The People's Guide to Congress.* New York: W.W. Norton, 1996. 164 pp. (JK1067.G74)

Hoig, Stan. *A Capital for the Nation.* New York: Cobblehill Books, 1990. 128 pp. (F194.3.H65)

Hutson, James H. *To Make All Laws: The Congress of the United States, 1789-1989.* Washington, D. C.: Library of Congress 1989. 120 pp. (JK1061.H86)

Kennon, Donald R., ed. *The United States Capitol: Designing and Decorating a National Icon.* Athens, Oh.: Ohio University Press, 1999. 316 pp. (NA4411.U55)

Leech, Margaret. *Reveille in Washington: 1860-1865.* New York: Harper and Brothers, 1941. 483 pp. (E501.L4)

Scott, Pamela. *Temple of Liberty: Building the Capitol for a New Nation.* New York: Oxford University Press,1995. 150 pp. (NA4412.W18S63)

Wolanin, Barbara. *Constantino Brumidi: Artist of the Capitol.* Washington, D.C.: Government Printing Office, 1998. 247 pp. (ND237.B877W65)

Websites: Visit www.uschs.org. and go to Links toconnect to a wide variety of Capitol Hill sites.

Index

We the People

of the United

insure domestic Tranquility, provide for the common defence, promote the ge
and our Posterity, do ordain and establish this Constitution for the United S

Article. I.

Section. 1. All legislative Powers herein granted shall be vested in a Cong
of Representatives.

Section. 2. The House of Representatives shall be composed of Members cha
in each State shall have Qualifications requisite for Electors of the most numerous Bra

No Person shall be a Representative who shall not have attained to the Ag
and who shall not, when elected, be an Inhabitant of that State in which he shall b

Representatives and direct Taxes shall be apportioned among the several State
Numbers, which shall be determined by adding to the whole Number of free Persons, in
not taxed, three fifths of all other Persons. The actual Enumeration shall be made
and within every subsequent Term of ten Years, in such Manner as they shall by La
thirty thousand, but each State shall have at Least one Representative; and until
entitled to chuse three, Massachusetts eight, Rhode-Island and Providence Plan
eight, Delaware one, Maryland six, Virginia ten, North Carolina five, South Ca

When vacancies happen in the Representation from any State, the Executiv
The House of Representatives shall chuse their Speaker and other Officers; a

Section. 3. The Senate of the United States shall be composed of two Senators fr
Senator shall have one Vote.

Immediately after they shall be assembled in Consequence of the first Ele
of the Senators of the first Class shall be vacated at the Expiration of the second Yea
Class at the Expiration of the sixth Year, so that one third may be chosen every second
Recess of the Legislature of any State, the Executive thereof may make temporary Appo
such Vacancies.

No Person shall be a Senator who shall not have attained to the Age of thir
not, when elected, be an Inhabitant of that State for which he shall be chosen.

The Vice President of the United States shall be President of the Senate, but sh
The Senate shall chuse their other Officers, and also a President pro tempore,
President of the United States.

The Senate shall have the sole Power to try all Impeachments. When sitt
of the United States, the Chief Justice shall preside: And no Person shall be convicte

Judgment in Cases of Impeachment shall not extend further than to rem
Trust or Profit under the United States: but the Party convicted shall nevertheless be
according to Law.

Section. 4. The Times, Places and Manner of holding Elections for Senator
thereof; but the Congress may at any time by Law make or alter such Regulation